Janette Marshall

A Dorling Kindersley Book

LONDON, NEW YORK, MELBOURNE,
MUNICH, AND DELHI

Senior Editor Dawn Henderson
Project Art Editor Anna Plucinska
Picture Research Louise Thomas
DTP Designer Adam Walker
Production Controller Sarah Dodd

Managing Editor Julie Oughton
Managing Art Editor Heather McCarry
Publishing Manager Adele Hayward

Art Director Peter Luff
Category Publisher Stephanie Jackson

Produced for Dorling Kindersley by
Renton & Johnston
World's End Studios
134 Lots Road London SW10 0RJ

For BBC Fat Nation:
Project Executive Charlotte Blofeld

Consultant Dr Susan Jebb (SRD)
MRC Human Nutrition Research

First published in Great Britain in 2004
by Dorling Kindersley Limited
80 Strand
London WC2R 0RL

A Penguin Company

2 4 6 8 10 9 7 5 3 1

Copyright © 2004 Dorling Kindersley Limited

**Always consult your doctor before starting a fitness and
nutrition programme if you have any health concerns.**

By arrangement with the BBC
BBC logo © BBC 1996
Fat Nation logo © BBC 2004
The BBC logo and Fat Nation logo are registered trademarks
of the British Broadcasting Corporation and are
used under licence.

A CIP catalogue record for this book is available from
the British Library.

ISBN 1 4053 0763 3

Colour reproduction by Colourscan, Singapore
Printed and bound by MOHN-Media, Mohndruck GmbH, Germany

Discover more at
www.dk.com

Contents

Introduction 6

Fill up or fuel up? 22

Time to get moving 36

introduction

Take one street of 200 residents, (well, two streets and a cul de sac!), show them the future, and ask them to be role models for the nation. That was BBC Television's answer to Britain's current obesity crisis.

Fat Nation – the Big Challenge wanted the residents of Greenway, The Croftway, and Garden Grove to lead the way in bringing exercise, good nutrition, and a healthy, balanced attitude to food to viewers right across the UK.

Fat Nation wanted to re-educate without being worthy and equip people to confront the obesity crisis and prevent the problem being passed on to their children and future generations.

But fun was on the menu as Fat Nation followed the fortunes of folk on an average British street as they went about their daily business.

big challenge

A team of experts moved in to the street to address each individual's health and fitness issues. They encouraged the street to eat in, work out, and examine their mind sets.

Weekly challenges (that you will find throughout this book) for the street and for the viewers proved that getting fit can be great fun and doesn't involve a lot of time, effort, or expense.

Using the experience on the street, and other examples of best practice in schools and communities around the country, Fat Nation showed millions of people how to adopt healthier behaviour patterns with the support of family, friends, and neighbours.

The advice and wisdom of the series, and more, has been distilled into this book. Along with tips and expert advice across all BBC television and radio channels, the BBC website, and interactive TV, it is part of a two-year BBC health campaign to make a difference to the nation's health – and weight. There's nothing to stop you now, so join in with the challenges, and good luck!

Turn on and tune in
About 24 million people in Britain are overweight or obese. Even if you are not one of them, you will know somebody with a weight problem – maybe as close as your partner or child. Changing eating and behaviour patterns along with the Fat Nation residents in the TV series is the first step to take. Then follow up with the information and fun activities in this book and from the BBC resources.
bbc.co.uk/bigchallenge

meet **the f-team**

Vicki Edgson (centre), Efua Baker (left), and Dr John Marsden are BBC1's Fat Nation F-team ("F" for fat!), who helped the residents of the Croftway to a healthier lifestyle.

Vicki raided the residents' fridges, throwing out junk food and cramming in healthier choices, Efua's innovative ways of making exercise enjoyable won over even the most sedentary of couch potatoes, and with his pragmatic approach to psychology, John helped residents find the willpower to make their diet and exercise dreams a reality.

The team agree that better health needs to suit your personal lifestyle. So, take the most fitting ideas from this book to help you carry on the work of the Fat Nation programme – and rise to the challenges!

You will also find some tips and words of encouragement from the F-team themselves in the expert photo-boxes (see right) throughout the book.

Good luck and keep going – it's worth it!

introduction 9

the size of the problem

One in four men and one in five women in Britain is obese. Being obese means being so overweight that your health is in danger. In the UK 900,000 people can't work because of obesity and at least 30,000 people die prematurely each year from obesity-related causes. Obesity shortens life by about nine years.

Levels of obesity have tripled since 1980, and there is no sign that the upward trend is slowing. Whereas the problem of excess weight and obesity used to be mainly in the over-45s, it is now affecting younger people and children. Being overweight increases the risk of many medical conditions, such as Type 2 diabetes, heart disease, and some cancers.

Scary stuff! But you have the power to do something about the problem. Whether you're a little overweight or a lot – change starts here.

Our Psychologist says:
Weight problems can be corrected, though some people will find it easier than others. Recognizing the benefits of a healthier lifestyle and realizing you can work towards a better quality of life is a big step in the right direction to losing weight and gaining more energy and zest for life.

fat

"Heading for disaster"

It is predicted that one in three adults and one in five children in the UK will be obese by 2020. In addition, there could be more than 1 million undiagnosed Type 2 diabetics whose condition has contributed to excess weight or obesity. In the view of the International Obesity Task Force, we are heading for disaster.

The health risks

Being overweight increases the risk of Type 2 diabetes, heart disease, high blood pressure, and other long-term diseases. These conditions are increasingly reported in younger people and children because of their weight problems. Weight-related long-term diseases can reduce life expectancy, or at best shorten the number of years sufferers could expect to live in good health.

Nowhere to hide?

Everyone is at risk of becoming overweight because it has such a simple cause: eating too much and not being sufficiently active. At face value, obesity should therefore be easy to remedy by eating less and being more active. The solution is not as simple as that. All aspects of life affect the amount and type of food we eat and our activity levels – for example education, income, transport, where we live and work, and leisure opportunities.

Time for change

Obesity is already reducing the quality of life for a growing number of people and costing the country more than £6billion a year. It is clear that something needs to be done – now. We can no longer accept overweight as the "norm".

We can do it!

The good news is that there is something that we as individuals can do. We can overcome or prevent weight problems. We can change what we eat. We can also learn how to eat less, eat better, and be more active in simple ways in everyday life.

Your guide to success!

Whether successful national strategies or policies emerge to overcome the nationwide obesity problem remains to be seen. But don't let yourself become part of the statistics in the meantime. This book is here to help guide you through the jungle of causes of your own weight problems (or those of a loved one). It will provide you with practical solutions and plans so that you can take matters into your own hands and embark on your personal success story.

Don't even start
As you may have noticed, gaining weight is easier than losing weight. Worse still, gaining weight just once makes the body more likely to gain weight a second and third time. And every time you put on weight, that weight becomes more difficult to shift. If you do not yet have a weight problem (lucky you!), your best course of action is to keep your weight controlled consistently. Piling on the pounds even once could set you on the slippery slope.

why we are **getting fatter?**

The simple explanation for the fact that Britain is gaining weight is that we are eating more "energy-dense" foods (foods that are relatively high in calories, mainly from fats) and that we are living an increasingly sedentary lifestyle. So, what went wrong?

To cut a long story short, we are biologically programmed to eat when food is available. Our Stone Age ancestors could only eat when they had been hunting and gathering, whereas all we have to do is drive to the supermarket.

In the 21st century, we live in a food-rich environment, and we have continued eating whenever food is available – which is most of the time in our 24-hour society. Eating has never been so easy!

simple

Fat chance to be slim

It's the cheapest foods – fast and convenience foods, sweets, and snacks – that tend to be the highest in calories. (These calories come from cheap fats, of the unhealthiest kind, and from manufactured sugars.) Because such foods are so energy dense, it's easy to eat what looks like the same size portion as a traditional meal without realizing that it contains far more calories. Supersize portions have made the problem worse.

Hooked on high calories

A taste for high-fat, high-sugar, and high-salt foods is easy to acquire and leaves a lot less space in your diet for more nutritious, lower-calorie foods. Trying to lose the taste for high-fat, high-sugar, and high-salt foods has been likened to kicking a drug addiction – it takes time and application, but use the motivational tips and practical plans available and you should lose weight successfully.

On the couch

Compared to 50 years ago, adults and children are less physically active and more sedentary at work, school, and in their leisure time. Advances in technology may be to blame, keeping us tied to computers, videos, and DVD players.

Social changes

Home-prepared and cooked foods are usually lower in calories than foods in restaurants, fast food outlets, and school and work canteens. But we are eating more food outside the home than ever before. (This may be due to a lack of time to prepare meals at home, a lack of cookery skills, or simply a lifestyle choice.) Eating fewer family meals and lack of a three-meals-a-day structure encourages overeating. And sometimes we don't think about what is going into our mouths – bolting down food on the run and supplementing meals with high-fat snacks and high-sugar fizzy drinks.

Mixed messages

While we undeniably need to be more active, the food industry has used this to muddle healthy eating messages encouraging people to eat less. Chocolate and fast food companies are keen to help sponsor physical activity schemes. "Healthy lifestyle" literature from the food industry implies that if you exercise enough you can eat what you like. The truth is that we all need to limit our food intake and most of us need to eat smaller portions, but the food industry would encourage us to continue eating "moderate" portions of non-nutritious foods.

Miss Chiplash says: The chances of becoming obese nearly double for each can or glass of high-sugar soft drink consumed every day. That's a good reason to lose the fizz.

how the body puts on weight

We all need to eat to live, but many people eat more than they need because food is so enjoyable. Which would be fine – if they burned off the calories. The trouble is, a sedentary lifestyle and habitually eating too much without making any adjustments at other times result in weight gain that can lead to obesity.

If you eat only the amount of food that your body needs, you burn it off and you don't gain weight. If you eat more calories than you burn, however, the extra energy is stored, first in the liver and then (when the store space in the liver is full) in different parts of the body in the form of fat.

it's a **simple rule**
(**calories in** = **calories out**)
= no weight gain

Why we overeat

Feeling hungry makes us eat, but our appetite needs to be switched off to stop us overeating and putting on too much weight. Hormones released by the intestines send signals to the brain, telling you not to go for second (or third) helpings. But many overweight people learn to ignore these signals and, over time, the signals can become blurred and go unrecognized. Our food-focused society and energy-dense foods make it too easy to overeat.

It's my genes!

This sounds like an excuse, but in some ways it's true. Your genes determine whether or not you gain weight easily. They also dictate where any excess weight is stored in your body – on your abdomen or your hips, for example – which has an influence on weight-related health problems. However, most people can "override" the influence of genes through healthy diet and adequate exercise. In other words, you do not have to put on weight.

Does eating fat make you fat?
All foods are potentially fattening if you eat them in large enough quantities, but fat contains more calories per gram than other food groups (see left). Calories from fat are also more likely to be deposited on the body as fat rather than burned off during physical activity.

energy value of foods

Fat contains more calories per gram than any other food group

Protein	4 calories per gram
Carbohydrate	3.75 calories per gram
Fat	9 calories per gram
Alcohol	7 calories per gram

BMR

The amount of energy or calories you need depends, for most people, on basal metabolic rate (BMR) and how active you are. The BMR is the amount of calories you use when your body is completely at rest. Men usually have a higher BMR than women. This is because a woman who is the same weight as a man has more fat and less muscle. Your BMR uses about two thirds of the calories you eat. Another 10 per cent is used to digest food and regulate body temperature – this leaves around 20 per cent for physical activity. The more active you are, the more calories you burn, and the less body fat you usually have. You can increase your physical activity to double your BMR. Exercise also keeps your metabolic rate at a higher level for some time after exercise, so you continue to burn more calories.

Our Psychologist says:
There's no need to feel despondent if you are carrying excess body fat – right here's where you can start to change. This book will help you to lose the fat and feel the benefits.

working **together**

If we are going to improve our health, both as individuals and as a society, and cut costs to the nation, we need to involve everyone. Whole communities, from school children to pensioners, need to understand the health problems associated with overweight and obesity and to make changes and support each other.

reasons to pull together

1 **the next generation** could have a shorter lifespan than the present

2 taking action will reduce the number of **obesity-related** conditions and demands on the health service

3 we can work with national and local planners to design **healthier communities** for "active" living

4 misleading **food labelling**, supersizing, and poor food will continue if we do nothing

5 lobbying en masse, is the only way to **force changes** in our obesity-promoting environment

Stop making excuses

We all have plenty of excuses for putting off until tomorrow our plans to lose weight and get fitter. But with the obesity "time bomb" of ill health acting as a national and international wake-up call, now is the time to get started. It's time to throw out our "I know I should" excuses and start thinking and acting more positively. Do it for you, do it for your family, and do it for your community.

Workplace awareness

Suggest anti-obesity initiatives at your place of work. Could your employer promote or reward active travel to work? What about a "ban the lift" day once a week in which everyone has to use the stairs? You could organize a Friday lunchtime kickabout in a nearby park. And is the canteen food healthy with low-fat options? If not – why not? After all, a healthy workforce is a happy (and productive) workforce.

here's a
radical thought!

Every day ask yourself – what can I do today to eat less and move more? Look for small ways to meet your goals all day, because every little step counts towards a better, fitter future.

a communal effort

- Babysit so that friends or neighbours have time for exercise
- Start a street football, netball, or swimming group
- Offer to go shopping for fresh food for elderly or house-bound neighbours
- Organize a walk-to-school "bus", where children walk in a group with an adult "driver"
- Ask the local doctor's surgery to plan some healthy-living talks
- Ask the borough to provide more playground equipment

Become a school governor

Schools are always in need of positive and supportive governors. You could work with your local school to help fund or organize healthy initiatives such as starting a school vegetable garden or overhauling the contents of the vending machine. And talk to the local authority about safe walking and cycling routes and play areas.

fancy-footwork challenge

You can burn loads of calories and increase your heart rate tangoing, do-si-do-ing, or throwing some shapes at the nightclub. Choose the steps, grab a partner (or three), and start tip-tapping your way to fitness. It's a great way to have fun with family, friends, and neighbours.

everybody's doing it

It is reassuring to know that you are not alone in your search for a solution to your weight and fitness problems. Across the nation, millions of people, of all ages and with many different lifestyles, are trying to lose weight and achieve a greater sense of wellbeing. Some of these people are going it alone, but for many people, tackling the problem as a family, organizing a support group among friends, or joining a weight-loss club can be a huge help and may be the key to success.

Miss Chiplash says: Cutting out just one biscuit a day could "save" you 100 calories a day. That adds up to enough calories to prevent the average annual 1kg (2.2lb) weight gain a year that happens to most adults. Whatever your age, make this change.

Singles

If you are focusing on your career, long hours at work can limit your time for getting fit. Finding a quick way to relax and de-stress after work may mean that you are a regular at the pub, followed by a takeaway. Or you may open the wine as soon as you get home from work and snack on crisps until your evening meal is ready. Lack of cooking skills or limited facilities in shared accommodation can compound the problem, making you over-reliant on convenience and fast foods. What can you do?

- Adopt at least one daily healthy meal habit. Eat breakfast, for example. A fortified cereal with skimmed milk is quick and easy.

- Shape up in your daily life. There are plenty of non-sporting ways to be active, including dancing, brisk walking, and shopping – during which you can walk miles.

- Keep an alcohol diary to see how many units a week you are drinking (see p136 for the recommended limits). Try exercising to unwind instead!

Busy mums

Motherhood is a time when some women gain weight. If you have very young children, disturbed nights may leave you lacking in energy, so that even the thought of taking physical exercise leaves you exhausted. You may also be in the habit of snacking with the children or eating up their leftovers, which can cause your weight to creep up. If your life revolves around babies and children, you may find that you have little time left to prepare healthy meals or get physical. But now it's time to think about you!

- Learn to put your children's leftovers in the bin where they belong. Repeat after me, "I am not a dustbin…".

- Become more active with the family. Push the buggy at a brisk pace, chase your children round the park, or take them swimming (and swim along too).

- Make a deal with your partner, a friend, or neighbour to regularly take it in turns to do some physical activity while the other person looks after the children.

My treat!
Reward yourself for any change in behaviour that you successfully keep up for a couple of weeks. Perhaps you have built 15 minutes more activity into your day – buy yourself a CD or a new T-shirt. Or maybe you are meeting the 5-a-day fruit and vegetable target – buy some luxury shower or bath products or some stylish stationery. Whatever you choose, always keep the focus of your rewards away from food.

you can do it

Empty nesters

You may have reached 50+ to find that middle-age spread has caught up with you. Are you eating the same quantity of food that you did when you were younger and more active? With age, calorie requirements decrease, so you need to eat less to stay the same weight. If you are in a job that requires a lot of travel or long hours at a desk or in meetings, you may be tempted by hospitality food and drink. Being away from home may also mean that eating is "something to do" or a comfort. Take steps to change.

- Cut down on less nutritious high-calorie foods, such as biscuits and fried foods. Replace them with fruit, larger servings of vegetables, or wholegrain breads.

- Regard the third age as a time when you can be fitter than you have ever been. You have lots of time to gradually work up to being a fit pensioner!

- Write down how many hours a day you spend sitting (you may be surprised) and then find ways to halve it.

start here to **change your life**

Losing weight to gain better health and more energy is not just a question of eating less. You need the full armoury of weapons of fat destruction if you are to win the battle! Your total commitment involves both mind and body. Diet alone is not enough to solve weight problems permanently. Physical activity and your mental commitment to the task are equally important.

Are you ready to join the nation in losing weight and gaining a better quality of life? It may be easier than you think – all you need to do is E.A.T. – Eat differently, by making healthier food choices; Act differently, by being more physically active; and Think differently, by changing your behaviour and staying motivated.

eat
act
think

Keep a diary

Keeping a daily food and activity diary for a typical week can help you identify patterns of behaviour and decide where you need to make changes. Every day, write down what you eat, and at what time. You could also log how hungry you felt before eating. And write down how much activity you do each day. Some diaries also include emotions (sad, lonely, angry, bad hair day) because these can lead you to overeat when you are not hungry (see p154 for an example of a food and activity diary).

Our Psychologist says:
Think about the many benefits of improving your diet and fitness. This book will show you how to "unlearn" unhealthy eating habits and use exercise as the key for a healthy and fun life. Let's get to it!

fill up or fuel up?

Eating to lose weight is all about choosing the **right fuel** for your engine. If you fill up on high-fat, high-sugar, and high-salt foods you will be sluggish and slow – going nowhere. But if you choose nutritious, healthy foods, you'll be a lean, mean machine, with enviable bodywork and a well-oiled gearbox. Get the **balance** right and you'll soon be revving your engine ready to keep burning off calories.

do you need to **lose weight?**

A useful way to find out if you need to lose weight is to measure your Body Mass Index (BMI). This is a better indicator of health than weight alone. Use the following steps to calculate your BMI. If you prefer to look up your BMI on a chart, turn to p151.

to calculate your BMI

1 measure your height
in metres

2 multiply this number
by itself

3 measure your weight
in kilograms

4 divide your weight by your height
squared (the answer to question 2)

5 check your results against
the table opposite

Are you an apple or a pear?

BMI cannot take into account distribution of fat, which is important in assessing health risks. Large hips, for example, pose less of a health threat than a "spare tyre". In women, excess fat tends to be deposited around the upper arms, breasts, and hips – resulting in a pear shape. Most overweight men tend towards abdominal fat.

- Measure your waist and hips in centimetres
- Divide the waist measurement by the hip measurement to get your waist–hip ratio

Male pears should have a ratio of less than 0.95cm, and female pears less than 0.87cm. Any higher than that means you're an apple, which is associated with health conditions.

How does your waist measure up?
Your waist measurement can also give you another useful indicator of your health. Women who have waist measurements of 81–88cm (32–35in) face increased health risks; more than 88cm indicates high risk of Type 2 diabetes and maybe heart disease. For men, health risks increase at 94–102cm (37–40in) and substantially increase beyond 102cm (41in).

what does your BMI mean?

< 18.5	Underweight
18.5–24.9	Ideal or healthy weight
25–29.9	Overweight
30–34.9	Obese
35–39.9	Very obese
40+	Extremely (morbidly) obese

Surprised by your BMI?

The BMI chart is a guide. Stocky or muscular people and adolescents during growth spurts might have BMIs that suggest they're overweight when they're not (see children's BMI pp152–153). Athletes have higher BMIs because of their dense muscle tissue. If you think your BMI is unrealistically high, appraise yourself honestly, or ask the opinion of your doctor. Some people have larger, heavier builds than others, and if you are one of them, it would be a mistake to try to lose weight unnecessarily. If you are physically fit, then you probably have no excess risk of diseases such as high blood pressure, heart disease, and stroke. On the other hand, be honest – if your BMI is too high because you are overweight, it is time to make changes to improve your eating and exercise habits.

eating to be **the right weight**

You don't need a special diet, or a crash diet, or any kind of diet to lose weight or maintain your ideal weight. What you need is a healthy, balanced diet as shown below.

the main **food groups**

fruit and
vegetables

bread, potatoes,
pasta,
and cereals

meat, fish,
and protein
alternatives

fatty and
sugary foods

milk, cheese,
and yoghurt

Putting food in groups

By eating the number of portions per day that matches your calorie needs, you can control your weight (provided you are also physically active enough). Although everyone's calorie needs differ, depending on their sex, age, and how active they are (see pp140–141), there are general daily guidelines for the number of portions from each food group that you can eat to maintain the correct weight. As a rule, fuel up on tasty, nutritious food that is naturally low in fat and keep high-fat and high-sugar "treats" to a minimum.

In the drink
You need to drink 1.5–2 litres, or 6–8 glasses of liquid a day, most of which should be water. For the sake of variety, however, you can supplement this with other drinks such as fruit juice, milk, tea, coffee, herb or fruit teas.

find a daily balance

Fruit and vegetables (5+ portions)

Eat a variety of fruit and vegetables. A portion is:

- 2 tablespoons cooked vegetables
- 1 piece of fruit
- 1 tablespoon dried fruit

Bread, potatoes, pasta, and cereals (5–11 portions)

Choose wholegrain versions where possible. A portion is:

- 1 slice of bread
- 1 medium potato
- 1 tablespoon breakfast cereal

Milk, cheese, and yoghurt (2–3 portions)

Choose low-fat options where possible. A portion is:

- 200ml milk
- 40g (1½oz) hard cheese
- 125g pot yoghurt

Meat, fish, and protein alternatives (2–3 portions)

Choose lean meat and go for low-fat options. A portion is:

- 60–90g (2–3oz) beef, pork, lamb, poultry, or oily fish
- 2 eggs (limit to 4 per week)
- 50g (2tbsp) nuts or seeds

Fats and oils (0–3 portions)

Keep fats to a minimum (see pp128–129). A portion is:

- 1 teaspoon butter, cooking oil, mayonnaise, or salad dressing
- 2 teaspoons low-fat spread

High-fat, high-sugar foods (0–2 portions)

Keep these foods to a minimum. A portion is:

- 1 packet crisps
- ½ chocolate bar
- 3–5 sweets

think **slim**

Stop eating while you still feel slightly hungry. You may well find that 20 minutes later, once you have started to digest your food, you actually feel satisfied. This is a useful practice that some people find effective in tackling weight problems.

Our Psychologist says:
Changing your behaviour will mean that increased physical activity and a healthy, varied diet become second nature after a while. But if you have the occasional lapse along the way, don't panic. Just think of it as a temporary glitch. Whether you stray off course for a few days or for weeks, it doesn't matter – just get back on track as soon as you can.

To change the way you relate to food and alter your eating habits, you need to start behaving more like a slim person, many of whom practise "restricted eating". For example, if a slim person eats a lot at one meal or on one day, he or she usually compensates by eating less at the next meal or on the following day.

Think about how you currently behave towards food, and then consider ways to change your behaviour. You may be in the habit of eating on "automatic pilot", without thinking about whether or not you are really hungry. Instead, engage your brain before reaching for food. Ask yourself "Am I hungry?" "Do I need this?" "Will I regret eating this?" "Am I about to eat because of an urge (mental craving for food) or because I am hungry?" Then act accordingly!

think first

Walk around temptation

Change your route to and from work, school, or the shops if you find you cannot go past the coffee shop without popping in for a latte and muffin, or past the chip shop without stopping and eating.

Plan your snack attacks

If the vending machine at work is sending you siren calls all day, take in pre-planned healthy snacks and keep them at the ready for those mid-morning hunger pangs.

Fuel yourself up first

If you tend to buy sweets or sugary drinks whenever you visit the garage to fill up your car, have a healthy nibble before, or keep healthy snacks in the car itself.

Keep a clear head

If drinking alcohol lowers your resistance to saying "no" to food and leads to overeating, drink less, or on fewer occasions. Alcoholic drinks can also be fattening in themselves, so doing this really will help to reduce your waistline.

Beware the fridge

If you're partial to nibbling on pieces of cheese or other high-fat bite-sized treats whenever you pass the fridge, replace them with healthy alternatives, such as fruit and low-fat yoghurts.

teach yourself new habits

Old behaviour

- Piling up your plate
- Having second helpings
- Eating in front of the TV
- Turning to high-fat comfort foods when under stress
- Snacking when you are bored

New behaviour

- Have a sensible portion
- Pass up on seconds
- Sit at the table to eat
- Try relaxation breathing techniques
- Phone a friend or go for a walk and forget about food

Are you ready for change ?

To make sure you have no doubts about making changes, ask yourself:

What is my level of interest in weight control and management?

- **a.** Not interested
- **b.** Interested
- **c.** Very interested

What is my goal?

- **a.** To look better
- **b.** To feel fitter
- **c.** Both

Am I ready to commit to lifestyle changes?

- **a.** Not ready
- **b.** Ready
- **c.** Can't wait

How confident am I that I can lose weight slowly and permanently?

- **a.** Unsure
- **b.** Confident
- **c.** Very confident

If I need to, will I seek moral support from family, friends, or a club?

- **a.** I'll go it alone
- **b.** Maybe
- **c.** Definitely

If you answered mostly a) or b), you may need more time to think about a healthier lifestyle – set a date for the future. Mostly c) – you're ready now, so go for it!

portion **distortion**

As the portion sizes of fast foods, convenience foods, pub and restaurant servings (and the amount of food we serve ourselves at home) have grown, so, too, have our waists.

Take burger and fries portion sizes, for example. Twenty years ago, you would have been served a 65g (2oz) portion of fries, containing around 200 calories. Today, a standard portion is nearer 200g (7oz), supplying 600 calories. Remember, eating just 100 calories a day more than you use means you put on 1kg (2lb) of weight a year.

It's this kind of "passive overeating", in which you think you are eating the same amount of food, but are in fact eating larger portions of energy-dense fatty or sugary foods, that is one of the major contributing factors towards Britain becoming a fat nation. It's time to downsize...

size matters

here's a
radical thought!

You could put on 0.5kg (1lb) of fat in a week if you drank just one large (full-fat) latte a day for 7 days. Putting on 1lb of body fat would take you 9 days if you drank 2 semi-skimmed large capuccinos every day. Swap to skinny lattes or capuccinos instead and keep the calories down.

Mustn't whine
Alcohol portions have also been supersized, so watch out. See pp136–137 for the new facts and figures.

Miss Chiplash says:
You thought the food manufacturer was your friend, giving you value for money, or even a free gift – buy a packet of sandwiches and get a free fizzy drink or packet of crisps or a chocolate bar. Avoid meal-deal lunch bargains and have a wholegrain sandwich and a piece of fruit or yoghurt.

fill up or fuel up? 31

using portions to **control weight**

Using portions to work out how much to eat in order to lose weight, or maintain your healthy weight, is far more relaxed, and much easier, than counting calories. It also ensures that your diet is balanced and full of beneficial nutrients from vitamins and minerals to keep you healthy.

when choosing your portions

1 choose low-fat, wholegrain **starchy** foods where possible

2 mix and match **fruit and vegetable** varieties, but try not to eat all fruit

3 opt for **lean meat, fish, poultry,** and low-fat protein alternatives

4 choose low-fat or "virtually fat free" **milk, cheese, and yoghurt**

5 keep **high-fat and high-sugar** foods to a minimum

Lose weight safely

To lose weight safely, it needs to be at a rate of around 0.5kg (1lb) per week. This may not seem a lot, but if you lose weight slowly, you are more likely to keep the weight off. To do this, you need to eat 500–600 fewer calories per day than the number of calories you use.

Your calorie requirements

Women lose weight eating 1200–1500 calories per day. Once you have lost the weight, sedentary women need to stick to a calorie intake of around 1800 calories a day (slightly less than the estimated 1940 calories a day recommended for adult women aged 19–49). Older women need fewer – 1900 calories. Young women and adolescents need 1845–2110 a day. Pregnant and adolescent women should not restrict their calorie intake.

Men lose weight on 1800–2000 calories per day. Once you have lost weight, you can increase your calorie intake to the estimated 2550 calories a day needed by most men aged 19–49. Older men need fewer – 2380 calories. Younger men and adolescents need 2220–2755 calories a day.

Calories to portions

Don't worry about counting the calories – you don't have to. Just stick to the portion guides below and on the following pages and you'll stay on track.

Take action

If you do about an hour of moderate activity every day, you will be able to eat well and keep your weight steady. Being active will speed up your weight loss and help to prevent you regaining weight.

Time to downsize
If you have previously chosen "megasize" or "kingsize" portions, you need to get into the habit of always asking for small or medium portions from now on – they really are just as satisfying.

weight loss with portions

Women	1200cals	1600cals	Men	1800cals	2000cals
Starch	6	7	Starch	8	10–11
Fruit	2	3	Fruit	3	4
Vegetables	3	3	Vegetables	4	4
Protein	1.5	2	Protein	2	2–3
Milk	2	2	Milk	2	3
Fat	1–2	3	Fat	4	4
Snacks (calories)	100	150	Snacks (calories)	200	250

tbsp=1 tablespoon

tsp=1 teaspoon

What is a portion?

If you are unsure about portion size, you may find it helpful to weigh or measure to gauge the size of a portion before you start. Once you are used to how a portion looks on your plate, you will be able to judge by eye. Below is a list of the food groups with the portions of specific foods within them. If you follow these guidelines (continued on pp155–156), you can plan your eating and control your weight.

meal portion options

Bread, potatoes, pasta, and cereals

These starchy foods should take up the largest proportion of your daily eating. You can choose from a variety of foods. Some portion options are:

3 tbsp breakfast cereal

3 tbsp porridge oats

2 tbsp muesli

1 slice of bread or toast

½ pitta or 1 mini pitta

1 small chapatti

½ bread roll or bagel

3 small crackers or crispbreads

1 medium potato

2 small new or salad potatoes

2 heaped tbsp boiled rice

3 heaped tbsp boiled pasta

3 heaped tbsp boiled noodles

1 medium plantain

1 medium sweet potato, or
1 medium piece of yam

Fruit and vegetables

Include at least 5 portions of fruit and vegetables in your daily diet – keep it varied and interesting:

3 tbsp cooked vegetables such as peas and carrots

1 side salad

1 tomato or 7 cherry tomatoes

1 medium piece of fruit (apple, medium banana, half grapefruit, or slice of melon)

3 heaped tbsp cooked or canned fruit (in juice or water, not syrup)

2–3 small fruits (plums, apricots, and satsumas)

1 handful of grapes

Milk, cheese, and yoghurt

Keep a check on these foods and go for low-fat options:

200ml (⅓ pint) semi-skimmed milk

30g (1oz) hard cheese (such as Cheddar)

Balancing act

Portion control is all about finding a good balance. Stick to the portions on pp–32–33 and you'll soon notice the difference. Choose wisely from the portion options to keep your menu exciting.

Snack attack

Snacks account for about a quarter of our total calorie intake, so they can have a huge influence on weight. Keep snacking healthy and count the calories. More snacks are listed on p155.

Stick to the portions on pp–32–33
More snacks are listed on p155.

Meat, fish, and protein alternatives

Protein doesn't always need to be meat – there are plenty of other sources. Mix it up:

60–90 g (2–3oz) cooked lean beef, pork, lamb, extra-lean mince, chicken, turkey, or oily fish (salmon, mackerel, herring, or sardines)

75–120g (3–4½oz) raw meat, poultry, or oily fish

2 thin slices lean cold meat

150g (5oz) cooked white fish or canned tuna (in brine or spring water)

120g (4½oz) soya, tofu, or vegetable-based meat alternative

Fats and oils

Keep fats and oils to a minimum and choose wisely:

1 tsp margarine or butter

2 tsp low-fat spread

1 tsp oil or ghee

1 tbsp mayonnaise or vinaigrette

snack facts

Approx. 50 calories

1 plain biscuit

1 medium piece of fruit

2 crispbreads

1 small pot virtually fat-free yoghurt

Approx. 100 calories

2 pieces of fruit

2 rice cakes with low-fat spread,

1 cereal bar

2 plain biscuits

Approx. 150 calories

1 small slice toast with low-fat spread

1 fruit bun or scone (no spread)

1 bread roll

Approx. 200 calories

2 slices bread or toast with spread

2 crackers with 25g (1oz) cheese,

3 tbsp breakfast cereal with 200ml (⅓ pint) skimmed milk

here's a *radical thought!*

Slim people tend to be frequent snackers, eating little and often and then compensating for snacking by reducing their food intake at meal times to balance out their total daily food intake. Some eat their food as 5 or 6 small meals during the day. If you try this, be careful because unless the meals are small, you could gain weight.

Miss Chiplash says: Instead of eating low-fat foods, you could try eating smaller portions of their full-fat alternatives. But I really do mean smaller portions! Check the nutrition labels to be sure.

time to.
get moving

Our sedentary lives are making us fat – we need to be **more active** to help us to control weight. Get off the sofa and find ways to increase your activity level in **daily life**. There are ways to burn off calories without even leaving the house! Better still, take up a new **sport** or **activity** to really get you moving on a regular basis.

your **body-fat percentage**

Being the right weight is not the whole story. The risks to health depend more on what proportion of your weight is fat than on how much you weigh. If your body-fat percentage is high, you need to take steps to reduce it for the sake of your health. Find out more about the specific health risks associated with excess body fat in Staying Healthy (pp116–137).

body-fat percentages

Sex/Age	Healthy	Fat	Obese
Women			
20–39	21–23	34–38	39+
40–59	23–34	35–40	41+
60–79	24–36	37–42	43+
Men			
20–39	8–20	21–25	26+
40–59	11–22	23–28	29+
60–79	13–25	26–30	31+

Ethnicity matters

As yet there is no agreed UK standard for body-fat percentages. However, leading experts in the UK have devised guidelines (as shown left) based on BMIs (see p25), but they specify that the figures probably differ slightly among ethnic groups. Asian races from the Indian subcontinent have the highest fat mass for their BMI, followed by Caucasians, then the Japanese, with Black Africans having the lowest. Bear your ethnic background in mind when you compare your body-fat percentage with the guidelines – you may have a little leeway either way!

How much fat do I have?

The most accurate way of finding your body-fat percentage is to go to your doctor for a scan. Or, you could use a body-fat monitor at the gym. This is a special type of bathroom scale. You feed in your weight, height, and age, then stand on the metal pads on the scales. An electric current is sent through your body (you don't feel a thing!) that measures your fat percentage. Or you could use a machine that reads from electrodes attached to your hand and foot. This type of machine usually provides details of your body-fat percentage, as well as a break down of fat in kg, lean tissue, and water. Ask at a local gym or consult your doctor for advice.

Metabolic matters

Many people say that they are fat because they naturally have "a slow metabolic rate". The reality is, however, that heavier people burn more calories than lighter people – it takes more energy to move a heavier body after all! By increasing the amount of physical activity you do, you'll raise your metabolic rate further, burning off more fat. The worst thing you can do for your metabolism is to go on a crash diet. This will slow your metabolism down as your body tries to conserve energy and, when you go back to "normal" eating, can lead to weight gain.

what's your %?

What does it mean?

Knowing your body-fat percentage is probably more useful than knowing your BMI because two people can have the same BMI, or weight, but the health risks, such as Type 2 diabetes, heart disease, and certain cancers, are higher for the person with the higher body fat percentage. So, even if your BMI falls within the recommended range, if your body-fat percentage is high, you need to take action.

What shall I do?

Action is the key word – the only way to guarantee fat loss is through a combination of physical activity and improved diet. If you just diet without taking exercise you will lose far less fat. So, follow the healthy fat-busting eating guidelines in this book and start moving towards a slimmer, trimmer you by taking opportunities to get physical. See pp144–149 for some practical fat-burning programmes.

It's not that simple!

The trouble is that when you lose weight you are not necessarily discarding pure fat. Aah… if only weight and fat loss were as simple as taking off a fat suit to reveal a slimmer, trimmer you. Weight loss, particularly on an unbalanced low-calorie diet, can be mainly water or glycogen (energy stored in the liver). The usual water and stored energy loss that occurs during the first week or so of a diet could account for as much as 3kg (6.5lb) of weight loss – but the fat itself is still there.

Too little body fat?

You may envy very skinny people, but it is also unhealthy to have insufficient fat on your body. Younger women who are too thin risk fertility problems and missing menstrual periods is common in women with low body fat. They are also at risk of anaemia and, in combination with too little calcium, they increase their risk of developing osteoporosis later in life. Having a sensible attitude to body fat is the way forward. What you need to achieve is a healthy body-fat percentage that is right for you.

take off the fat

Let's get physical

When you exercise, you raise your basal metabolic rate (BMR), the rate at which you burn calories, so taking exercise means that you burn more calories than you do when you are sitting around. After exercising, your BMR remains high for a while and you can continue to burn more calories for a few hours. Some forms of exercise are better for calorie burning than others. Some specific types seem to raise your BMR particularly high, so that you can continue to burn calories at an increased rate for up to 20 hours after exercising.

Best for BMR

To keep your BMR higher for longer, try interval training. After warming up, you train for short periods at high intensity then drop back to a steady pace before raising the intensity again. Resistance training is another BMR-boosting activity. You do repetitive muscle toning exercises using your body weight or gym equipment as resistance. For example, you could do lunges, chest presses, or press ups. Resistance training also builds muscle, which gives you greater potential to burn more calories and fat and thus lose weight.

fight fat by

1 eating **fewer calories** than you need and being more active

2 doing **moderate exercise** such as a brisk 30-minute walk on most days of the week

3 raising your **metabolic rate** by eating five or six small meals a day

4 **working out** at around 60 per cent of your maximum heart rate (see pp144–9)

5 doing **resistance (weight) training**, to build muscle to replace body fat

Why don't I lose body fat when I exercise so hard? A lot of people become frustrated about not burning off fat despite working themselves to a sweaty frenzy at the gym, or out running, or using equipment at home. In a nutshell, if you work too hard, you won't burn fat. After a period of time, your body gets used to doing its set exercise routine, and becomes more efficient at saving energy while doing it, so your weight or fat-loss and body-shape improvements slow down or stop. You need long, slow distance training to increase your aerobic threshold in order to burn fat.

Seeing the benefit

By exercising, you can raise your BMR from around 1500 calories a day to 1800 calories a day. This means that you will burn off an additional 300 calories a day, which adds up to a whopping 2100 calories a week. This is around 0.5kg (1lb) of fat per week! Think of it another way. If your friend has a sedentary lifestyle, he or she is likely to have the lower BMR (1500), but he or she may eat 1800 calories a day. You may also eat 1800 calories a day, be the same age and sex as your friend, but by exercising and raising your BMR to 1800, you're tipping the scales in your favour. Who is going to put on weight? Your friend is and you are not.

do you need to be more active?

Most people today have a sedentary lifestyle through no fault of their own…but people who manage to keep their weight in check are physically active. Being active is as important as what you eat, and how much you eat, in successful weight control.

Being more active will help you

1 **maximize fat loss** in the weight that you lose

2 **increase your muscle** to fat ratio, changing your shape and toning you up

3 **suppress your appetite** and also burn more calories

4 **improve your mood** and reduce your stress level

5 **lower your cholesterol level** and the risk of heart disease

Don't just sit there!

Adults with a sedentary lifestyle spend most of their work and leisure time sitting down. If this is you, you need to do more than 30 minutes of moderate activity a day to control your weight. One hour is the prescription if you are sedentary and you need to lose or not gain weight.

What counts as activity?

Many everyday activities count as moderate exercise, so you don't have to join a gym or an exercise class (unless you would like to) to work your body. Find a moderate activity – one that leaves you slightly sweaty and breathless but able to speak coherently. As you get fitter, you can be more vigorous!

How active are you ?

How many times a week do you do any of the following: housework; gardening; walking; swimming; cycling; jogging; other workouts?

- **a.** Never or rarely
- **b.** One to four times
- **c.** Five or more times

In a typical day, how much time do you spend doing the above things?

- **a.** less than 15 minutes
- **b.** 15–30 minutes
- **c.** More than 30 minutes

When you take physical activity how do you feel?

- **a.** I don't get out of breath or sweaty
- **b.** I breathe easily but faster than normal
- **c.** I breathe faster and sweat but can talk easily

If you answered mostly a), you need to find ways of becoming more active. If you answered mostly b), keep up the good work and strive for c). If you answered mostly, c), well done, and keep up the good work – stay active!

choose your activity

Moderate activity

- Walking briskly
- Walking downstairs
- Dancing cheek-to-cheek
- Cycling on flat terrain
- Swimming
- Working in the garden
- Doing the housework

Vigorous activity

- Jogging
- Walking upstairs
- Dancing the salsa
- Cycling uphill
- Doing aerobics
- Rope skipping in the garden
- Playing a sport

Every little counts

Whether you are aiming for 30 minutes or a full hour of activity, you can break down your daily total into several short bouts, so that they are easier to achieve. One hour's exercise, for example, could be a brisk 20-minute walk, 20 minutes spent cleaning the car, and 20 minutes doing the housework. Smaller units of 10 minutes also "count", such as playing with the children in the park, climbing up and down the stairs, or dancing.

Tips for couch potatoes

Don't sit on the sofa and change the TV channel using the remote control (which uses 1 calorie), get up to do it (using 3 calories). Even ironing in front of the TV burns some energy – remember, it all adds up and can count towards your 30 minutes to one hour of activity!

being active in your **daily life**

To tackle the nation's growing weight problem, adults need to take 30 minutes of moderate activity a day to prevent weight gain and health problems. Activity can be part of daily living such as brisk walking, climbing stairs, and gardening. It can also include structured exercise as you progress.

take advantage of opportunities

1 get off the **bus or train** a stop earlier and take a brisk 10-minute walk or cycle to work

2 at work, use the **stairs instead of the lift**, and pop out for a walk at lunchtime

3 **visit your colleagues** at their desks with any queries, instead of calling them on the phone

4 at home, don't send the children around the house on errands to fetch and carry, **do it yourself!**

5 do household chores with **extra vigour** and have an indoor workout as you clean

Controlling your weight

To prevent weight gain, most adults need to do at least 30 minutes of moderate activity per day. Children need to do more (see p54). If your lifestyle is sedentary and you are overweight then around one hour of moderate activity daily is needed. Obese people will need to do 60–90 minutes daily to lose weight and improve health, in conjunction with a balanced diet. Moderate activity is aerobic because it raises the heart rate so you are aware of your pulse; it increases breathing and makes you feel warm or slightly sweaty.

Doing it your way

This is not about spending hours in the gym, although you can if you like, but don't feel guilty for not "working out". The idea is to find an activity that you want to do, coupled with becoming more active in your daily life. Ideal activities include walking, swimming, or cycling, although time spent doing housework, shopping, and general chores also counts towards your daily total. Even light activities such as ironing and dusting can help you to burn double the calories that you would sitting still.

be more active

If you are starting from scratch, begin with light activities. Your goal is to progress to more moderate activities on a daily basis.

Light activities

- Ironing
- Cleaning and dusting
- Walking, strolling
- Cooking
- Light gardening
- Shopping

Moderate activities

- Vacuuming
- Walking briskly
- Tennis (doubles)
- Mowing the lawn
- Badminton
- Golf

Improve your fitness

Moderate intensity activity makes you fitter, strengthens bones, and can be sustained for quite a long time without tiring you out. It also burns calories to help weight loss and prevent weight gain. The government advice is to exercise moderately for 30 minutes, five times a week. The table above shows how you might achieve that.

start **walking**

Walking is one of the easiest ways to control your weight and achieve your goal of being physically active every day. The World Health Organisation recommends one hour per day of moderate activity, such as walking, to maintain a healthy body weight, particularly for people with sedentary occupations.

So when you need to travel walkable distances (a mile or less), aim to walk rather than take the bus or car. Most people should aim to walk briskly at a pace of 6.4 kilometres per hour (4mph). If you are not used to walking, warm up by walking slowly to begin with and then picking up speed, and warm down at the end of your walk by reducing the pace. Go on – step out!

in your st

ide

walking challenge

It's the exercise that costs nothing, is safe, comfortable, and easy, yet few adults achieve the recommended daily 10,000 steps a day. Try mapping out a variety of walking routes in your local area and get friends and family involved – step out together!

setting and achieving **goals**

Setting goals is important. Without them you are in danger of being full of good intentions but having no practical plan of action. To control weight, your goal is one hour of moderate activity every day. Add to that at least another hour of activity per week, and you will meet your weight-loss and fitness targets.

take control

how active are you?

Inactive?

If you always drive or use public transport, are mainly sedentary, do minimal household and garden activities and take no active recreation, start by being more energetic in your daily life.

Do some housework and gardening and put some effort into walking part of the way to work. If you are home-based, go out for walks during the day, walk to a further postbox, and walk to the shops. At work, get up from your desk for walks at regular intervals in the day and take a good long walk at lunchtime.

Lightly active?

If you do some walking, cycling, light lifting and carrying, undemanding household and garden work, or a light-intensity recreation activity, then you need to step things up further.

Use your lunch hour to go for a brisk walk, or even a swim or a short gym session. Take shopping trips on a bicycle. Be more energetic about household chores, such as vacuuming and dusting, by stepping up your pace. Wash and wax the car instead of going to the car wash. You could also take up an active hobby or sport.

here's a
radical thought!

Make it part of your goal to be as fit as you were 10 years ago. If you weren't fit then, start now and aim to be twice as fit in 10 years' time. Age is no barrier to fitness – an active 60 year old is fitter than a sedentary 20 year old!

Golden rules

To be successful, your activity goals have to fit your life. Plan when and where you will walk or do your other physical activities and, maybe, with whom. Would it suit you to take exercise before work, during the working day, or after work? Make a decision and stick with it. Keep an activity diary and note down your weekly goals. If you need to take a swimming costume and towel, trainers, or a gym bag with you, remember to check you have it before you leave the house – why not stick a reminder note on the front door?

What are you aiming for?

Your aim is to be as active as you can and there are several ways you can do this. Take a daily walk or bike ride, to and from work or for leisure. Seize every opportunity to be active by using the stairs instead of taking the lift, for example. During the week, aim for two to three sport, gym, exercise class or swimming sessions. At weekends take longer walks, hikes, cycle rides, or a sports activity. If you have not done exercise classes before, look for classes that work at a steady low speed and do not require too much coordination!

Chart your progress
Mark on a calendar or in your diary the days on which you plan to take specific activities and then tick them off afterwards. You could use your own personal colour code, putting a red star, for example, on each day and then ticking it off if you manage to achieve at least 30 minutes of moderate activity. Then, on two or three other days, you could mark a blue star for extra activities such as more energetic housework or gardening, attending a class, or going to the gym. Aim to have at least 5 ticked red blobs and 2 blue blobs per week.

Moderately active?

Well done – you have already reached the recommended level. Maybe you commute regularly on foot or by bicycle. You may have a job such as a postman or a decorator, or do regular energetic household and garden activities – and do a moderate intensity sport or leisure activity on a regular basis.

Your task is to stay as active as you are as this level of physical activity is the best way of burning calories and losing fat. If you want to improve your fitness level, however, increase the duration and intensity of your activities.

Very or highly active?

You regularly do vigorous or very vigorous fitness training, possibly to maintain a competitive sporting activity. You probably commute on bicycle or foot or have a very active job such as labourer, farm worker, or gardener. You may also do regular heavy household or DIY garden and building jobs.

While you enjoy maximum fitness, you still need to look after yourself. Physical activity at this level carries a greater risk of injury, so include days when you are less active. Why not help someone else get fit, too?

up **a step**

As you become fitter, you may feel you want more of a challenge in your active life and to increase your speed, distance, or resistance. The body becomes accustomed to the same exercise routine and, to improve your fitness, you need to work at a higher level of intensity.

ways to be even more active

1 **mix it up** and or choose activities that exercise different muscles all over your body

2 **step it up** when you are ready and increase the time that you do your activity

3 **aim higher** once your body has become used to an activity, and step up the pace

4 **fuel fitness** and get the most from your active life with a balanced diet and plenty of water

5 **join a club or gym** that matches all of your physical (and financial) needs

Going it alone

If you like going it alone and have come to enjoy jogging, cycling, or running then you can use the streets or roads where you live or work and go out whenever an opportunity arises or it suits you.

In a group

If you prefer the consistency of an indoor environment and the variety of classes and gym work, try an affordable local leisure centre, club, gym, or college or school.

Gym advantages

The advantage of a gym or club is that you can be assessed by exercise professionals who will then set up a fitness programme tailored to your needs. Clubs also have a variety of machines, classes, and swimming facilities so that you can be sure that you are working your whole body and achieving all-round fitness. Some clubs have a free trial period for a week, so you can decide whether it will work for you before committing to a long-term contract.

three simple stretches

Make sure you stretch after exercise to avoid sore muscles. As you continue to be more active, you will soon find that muscle soreness will improve.

The hamstring stretch

- Stand with your feet together facing forwards
- Bend one leg at the knee and extend the other leg out straight in front, resting the heel on the ground with the foot flexed and the toes pointing up
- Lean forward slightly with your hands resting lightly on your thighs, but keep your head and chest raised
- Hold for around 30 seconds and repeat with your other leg

The calf stretch

- Stand on a step or a book and allow your heels to hang over the edge
- Gently lower your heels so that you feel a stretch in your calf muscles
- Hold for 30 seconds, then repeat

The front-thigh stretch

- Stand on one leg, holding a wall for support with one hand
- With the other hand, reach behind you and gently raise your other foot by holding your ankle
- Gently pull the foot towards your bum to feel the stretch
- Hold for 30 seconds and repeat with your other leg

Our Fitness Expert says:
If you have come this far you have done well. You are probably now feeling much more in control of your weight and at the recommended level of activity and you have decreased the risks to your health. You can now fine tune your goals to losing those final few pounds of weight.

keeping **on track**

When it comes to being active, staying motivated is probably more difficult than getting started. It's easy to start with lots of enthusiasm for a new regime, but harder to keep going, especially when you are busy, tired, or the weather is bad.

ways to stay motivated

1 make a date to **swim with a friend** – and stick to it

2 go out with a **walking group** and let the others set the pace

3 offer to **babysit** for some lively children – you'll be guaranteed an active evening

4 arrange to **take a friend's dog for a walk** and play a game of "fetch"

5 **book an exercise class** in advance and put it in your diary as an important date

Keep a diary

Setting aside time in your diary each week for physical activities is one way to stick at it. Writing down, in black and white, your commitment to exercise will keep you motivated. Paying in advance for classes in an aerobic activity of your choice – or even for a couple of sessions with a personal trainer – is money well spent and you'll be sure to keep your date if you've already parted with the cash.

Social sport

If you can play a social sport such as tennis, golf, squash, badminton, football, or netball, dust off your skills (maybe have a few lessons) and join a local club or find partners at a local leisure centre. Playing with others ensures you have the added incentive of having a date with someone and making it a social event. And someone is relying on you – you can't let your partner or opponent down.

Fun with gadgets
Special equipment or gadgets can increase your motivation. A pedometer (see p47) can be effective. Or invest in a heart-rate monitor (wristwatch and chest strap), allowing you to work within specific heart-rate zones, ensuring you burn fat and save yourself wasted energy – very satisfying! Or you could splash out and buy some home gym equipment, such as a treadmill or a stationary bike.

bringing the benefits home

Finding different ways to stay active is not that difficult when you look for them, especially if they offer other rewards:

- Spring clean your home
- Clean out your wardrobe
- Scrub the stains off the carpet
- Paint the walls of your house
- Clean your windows
- Mow the lawn
- Weed the garden
- Clip the shrubs or hedges
- Sweep the path and patio
- Bag up and throw out the rubbish
- Decorate a room in your home that needs a lift

Sponsored events

Undertake a sponsored event to raise money for a good cause – a local school or hospice. This will give you an incentive to train, to push yourself a bit harder, and to keep going. You could try a 5km race, a swimathon, or even a mini-triathalon – but give yourself plenty of time, around six to eight weeks, to prepare safely.

Become a trail blazer

Holidays spent backpacking, walking, and rambling (at home and abroad) are cheap and healthy. In summer, take a coastal cliff-top walk and blow the cobwebs away. In winter, book a weekend away at a hotel with a gym and a spa room for a luxurious, active retreat. It may be snowing outside, but you can still work up a sweat!

Our Psychologist says:
Keeping going is about celebrating your achievements – and enjoying life. When the going gets tough, look ahead and remind yourself of what you are working towards – a slimmer, fitter future. Remind yourself of the reasons for wanting to change and seek encouragement from family, friends, or professionals.

shopping for health

It's time to overhaul your **shopping habits** so that you always leave the supermarket armed with the **best food choices** for healthy eating. Take pleasure in leaving all the unhealthy foods that threaten to scupper your best intentions firmly **on the shelf**. Use the **quick and easy** golden rules for smart shopping and you certainly won't go off your trolley.

bad fridge

Keeping the whole family happy, shopping on a budget, and lack of time to browse the supermarket aisles, can result in a fridge full of salty convenience foods, fatty snacks, and sugary drinks. If this is your fridge, it's time for a shake up.

Flavoured and sweetened fruit drinks may look healthy, but they contain little real fruit juice and have poor nutritional value. Replace them with fresh fruit juice

Sweet treats are OK, sometimes, but put them at the back of the fridge, so that you don't automatically reach for them whenever you open the door. Keep fruit on hand instead

Fatty meats may be cheap, but you are paying for fat rather than meat when you buy sausages, salami, and streaky bacon. Replace them with lean meat and fish

Miss Chiplash says: Clearing out your fridge is so easy and can be very satisfying – giving you a clean sheet on which to build your healthy eating plan. So – if in doubt, chuck it out!

good fridge

Stocking up your fridge with healthy, fresh food can be easy and inexpensive and gives you the best chance of achieving a balanced diet. Start by clearing out your fridge and planning ways to make healthier choices.

You can have a healthy, low-fat meal ready in minutes with ready-to-use ingredients, such as fresh pasta and a jar of pesto or vegetable-based sauce

Place ready-cut fruit, vegetables, and low-fat yoghurts near the front of the fridge, so that any opportunistic snacking will be healthy snacking

A glass of unsweetened fruit juice counts as one of your five-a-day portions of fruit and vegetables, so stock up!

let's **go shopping**

You can have the healthiest intentions in the world when you set out to do the food shopping, but walking through the crisp and savoury snack section or dashing down the biscuit aisle can prove just too tempting. Stay smart.

golden rules for healthy shopping

1 try not to shop when you are **hungry, stressed or tired**, as you will blow your best intentions

2 compile a **basic shopping list of everyday foods** and get into the habit of buying them every week

3 have a rough idea of what **main dishes** you are going to cook over the following week

4 **familiarize yourself** with the shop layout so that you can avoid the aisles you don't need to go down

5 go for **fresh foods** where possible – they are usually the most healthy

Burn calories as you shop

If the supermarket you use has a fitness trolley that has gym machine technology, allowing you to make it harder or easier to push, then have a go. You can work out as you shop – in a 40-minute shopping trip at level 7, you can burn 280 calories, equivalent to a 30-minute jog.

Beware coupons and offers

Don't use money-off coupons or discounted price offers, unless you were already planning to buy those products or unless they are good nutrition and health value. Not many are, and you may end up buying something you don't really need or want.

Say "no" to BOGOF
Buying "three for two" or "supersize" portions is going to make it difficult not to overeat. These offers are often on the least nutritious foods (filled with the cheapest ingredients) such as biscuits, pizzas, snacks, and high-sugar breakfast cereals. Be a super shopper and say "no".

your healthy trolley

load up on...

- Lean meat – if buying fattier meat choose 5–10% fat mince, and extra-lean sausages and burgers
- Fresh fish – white and oily
- Bread – choose wholemeal and wholegrain
- Skimmed milk
- Low-fat yoghurt and low-fat fromage frais and crème fraîche
- Brie, edam, ricotta, and cottage cheese
- Fresh fruit juice
- Brown rice and wholemeal pasta
- Fresh fruit and vegetables – buy everyday items, such as apples and carrots, as well as special items, such as mango and aubergines

limit...

- Meat pies, pâté, sausages and salami
- Crumbed or batterered fish
- White bread and buns
- Full-fat milk, yoghurt, and hard cheese
- Fruit juice made with sugar and preservatives
- Gâteaux, iced cakes, chocolate fudge cake, cream cakes, and cheesecake

fridge challenge

Have you any idea what's lurking in your fridge and cupboards? There are evil things in there. Things that should never see the light of day. It's time to clear out your compartments and restock the shelves with healthy, nutritious ingredients fit for the trim, slim you.

front label

Beware the label! The houmus that claims to have "30 per cent less fat" than standard still contains 18g per tub and the garlic bread bearing the supermarket's "healthy eating" logo screaming "25 per cent less fat" still contains 14 per cent – around 24g of fat. Ouch!

It doesn't take a genius to work out that "less than 5 per cent fat" probably means 4.9 per cent fat – still too high to be healthy

When labels claim that a food is 95 per cent fat free, you might pop it in the trolley thinking it is "slimming". However, it still contains 5 per cent fat, so it is not actually "low fat'". A food is low fat when it contains 1.5–3 per cent fat

LESS THAN 5% FAT

95% FAT FREE

NUTRITION INFORMATION

TYPICAL VALUES	Per 100g	Per 40g serving
ENERGY VALUE	1532kJ/ 362kcal	613kJ/ 145kcal
PROTEIN	10.3g	4.1g
CARBOHYDRATES	67.2g	26.9g
of which sugars	21.9g	8.8g
FAT	5.8g	2.3g
of which saturates	0.8g	0.3g
FIBRE	6.9g	2.8g
of which soluble	1.7g	0.7g
of which insoluble	5.3g	2.1g
SODIUM	0.17g	0.07g

INGREDIENTS Wholewheat, rolled oats, raisins (12.5%), sugar, dried skimmed milk, dried milk whey, mixed sliced nuts (3%) (hazelnuts, almonds), malted barley extract, salt

CONTAINS: GLUTEN, COW'S MILK, NUTS

Scour the nutrition label at the back of the packet to make sure you are going for the healthiest option. If there is no list – you're already in trouble. The mysterious food is very likely high in fat, sugar, or salt – or all three!

Energy is expressed as calories (kcal) or joules (kJ). Men aged 19–50 years need about 2,550 calories per day, and women, about 1,940 calories per day

Protein - Men should be eating about 70g per day, and women, 50g

Carbohydrate – Men should eat around 340g per day, and women 240g. Choose less than 5g per 100g of sugars; the other type of carbohydrate is starch, which is healthy

Fat – Men should eat no more than 95g per day, and women 70g. Choose 1.5–3g or less per 100g and less than 1.5g per 100g of saturated fat

Dietary fibre - Men and women should eat 18g per day. Choose products with more than 3g per 100g

Sodium – To convert sodium to salt, multiply by 2.5. Men should eat no more than 7g of salt per day, and women, 5g. Choose products that contain 0.1–0.3g per 100g

don't be fooled by the label

If you are trying to control your weight and protect your health, you are going to have to scrutinize food labels and not take them at face value. Treat claims such as "low fat", "reduced sodium", and "high fibre" with care. There are few legal definitions and while the claims should not be misleading, the truth is they can be and they frequently are.

Food ingredients, including additives, are listed in descending order of weight. Take note, also, of "use-by" dates and follow storage, preparation, and cooking instructions to avoid food poisoning.

Miss Chiplash says:
Sugar may be listed as sugar, brown sugar (such as demerara, muscovado), or white sugar. Honey is a sugar, too. Simple. But did you know that all of the following are also names for sugars? Corn syrup, dextrin, dextrose, fructose, fructose syrup, fruit sugar, glucose, glucose syrup, invert syrup, maltose, sucrose, treacle, molasses, palm sugar, golden syrup, and maple syrup.

to buy or not to buy

A LOT per 100g	A LITTLE per 100g
More than:	Less than:
• 10g sugar	• 2g sugar
• 20g fat	• 3g fat
• 5g saturates	• 1g saturates
• 1.25g salt	• 0.25g salt
• 0.5g sodium	• 0.1g sodium

The calorie question

If you are choosing between two foods, such as breakfast cereals, and both have the same calorie content, compare the fat and carbohydrate content, then the vitamin and mineral content, to find the most nutrient-dense calories. Always go for the least energy-dense option – the cereal with the least fat and sugar and most starch, vitamins, and minerals. This simple rule can be applied to all packaged foods.

Get your fats straight

Packets of crisps that state "33 per cent less fat" may look healthy, but still contain around 22 per cent fat. Foods that shout "92 per cent fat free" contain 8 per cent fat. Food is low fat when it contains 3 percent fat, or less. The type of fat is important too: choose unsaturated in preference to saturated.

Buy bulk

Fibre fills you up, aids digestion, and also prevents constipation, haemorrhoids (piles), and more serious bowel problems. Where there is a choice, go for the higher-fibre product that's more than 3g per 100g.

Spot the salt

Sodium in processed foods, such as soups, pies, bacon, readymeals, and Chinese takeaways, comes mostly from salt, but may also come from food additives such as flavouring, monosodium glutamate (MSG), preservatives, and baking powder. Most of us are consuming far too much salt without realizing it, so keep your eyes peeled and choose low-sodium and low-salt foods and avoid salt-laden additives.

Complex or simple?

Choose the biscuits or bread (and other foods) in which most of the carbohydrate content comes from unprocessed (wholegrain) starch as opposed to sugar. Starch is complex carbohydrate, the healthy high-fibre type that keeps you feeling fuller for longer. Sugar is a simple carbohydrate, which gives you an instant but short-lived energy boost. It can leave you craving another sugary food soon afterwards and is devoid of nutrients, making it the ultimate "empty" calorie.

look and learn

shopping for **convenience foods**

Britain eats more than half of Europe's readymeals. Lack of time to prepare and eat meals, longer working hours, and commuting may be factors that lead you to go for the easy option. Most convenience foods are, however, high in fat, sugar, and salt.

making readymeals healthier

1 serve pasta- and rice-based readymeals with a **mixed salad and ratatouille**

2 beef up cottage and shepherd's pie by serving with **two portions of vegetables**

3 find a balance for fish pies, fish fingers, and fish cakes with **heaps of green vegetables**

4 eat Indian readymeals with a **vegetable serving and plain boiled rice or a naan**

5 serve Chinese readymeals with **plain boiled rice or boiled noodles**

Choose carefully

Try not to eat convenience foods more than once a week. When you do buy them, however, it's important to read the nutrition labels (see pp60–63) so that you don't get caught out. Pay particular attention to the fat, sugar, and salt content – and go for the reduced options whenever possible.

Serves how many?

You may find that a pack of food gives no indication about how many servings it contains – there may be enough calories for two, but one person might easily be able to eat the dish. Put the meal in the context of the rest of your day and gauge how much to serve yourself.

best-choice convenience puddings

- Fresh fruit served with low-fat fruit yoghurt
- Canned fruit (in water rather than syrup)
- 1 small scoop of low-fat ice cream with fresh fruit or a fruit compôte
- Low-fat sorbet or low-fat frozen yoghurt

- 1 small slice of fruit tart with vanilla or natural low-fat yoghurt
- Low-fat mousse or fool
- Reduced-fat Danish pastry or gâteau
- Meringue nest with fresh berries or compôte

Pass on the salt

Salt is a big problem when it comes to convenience foods. Many readymeals contain more than 40 per cent of the recommended maximum daily salt intake – and that's just one meal. Look for low-salt readymeals and "no added salt" convenience foods, such as canned vegetables, fish, and soup. Choose vegetables and fish canned in fresh water rather than brine. Check the labels of convenience foods to try to find ones that contain 0.3g or less of sodium per 100g. So called "healthy eating" meals often contain almost as much salt as standard meals and some contain even more than half your daily intake. Sausages can be extremely high in salt – far above the recommended amount for children (see p85). As with other convenience foods, serve them very infrequently.

Control your fat and salt
Eating more freshly prepared food will give you the opportunity to reduce the fat and salt in your diet and to control your weight and health better. If you need some help with healthy cooking techniques and ideas see pp74–77.

takeaway **meals**

Takeaway foods can make you unintentionally put on weight because they are high in fat and calories. Weight for weight, takeaways and fast foods typically contain 1 ½ times more calories than a home-cooked meal of "meat and two veg".

takeaway damage limitation

1 **before you visit** a fast food chain or order a takeaway, check online for the best menu choices

2 go for **low-fat, low-calorie** options, avoiding creamy sauces and deep-fried foods

3 **refuse the supersize** or "buy one get one free" offers – stick to a standard portion

4 **don't over-order** – think about how much you would eat for a healthy home-cooked meal and act accordingly

share food with friends instead of finishing it off yourself – they'll share your calorie intake too!

Batter and base

If you are having takeaway fish and chips, try not to eat all of the batter, because it soaks up fat during cooking. Find a chip shop that uses vegetable oil instead of animal fat, if possible. Choose thin-based pizza rather than deep-pan and opt for lean ham, seafood, or vegetable toppings – without cheese.

Who's calling you a killjoy?

You may fear that friends and family will feel threatened if you go all healthy on them, but you are not a killjoy or a party pooper. If you eat a balanced diet on a long-term basis, a few excesses when you order a takeaway at the weekend or for a special occasion will not have a serious impact on your weight.

Salt and fizz
Because takeaway foods often contain so much salt, you may be tempted to buy a fizzy drink to enjoy with your meal. These high-sugar drinks won't quench your thirst effectively, however, and they will make you put on weight. Drink water instead.

takeaway swaps

chinese whispers

- Sesame prawn toasts (70cals)
  swap for prawn crackers (15cals)
- Spare ribs (140cals)
  swap for spring roll (120cals)
- Chicken with cashew nuts (500cals)
  swap for chicken chop suey (360cals)
- Egg fried rice (200cals)
  swap for steamed rice (120cals)
- Four crisp duck pancakes (650cals)
  swap for stir-fried beef, peppers and black bean sauce (350cals)

burger bites

- Halfpounder or two in a bun with cheese (800cals)
  swap for plain burger in a bun or quarter pounder (500cals)
- Caesar salad with croutons and dressing (420cals)
  swap for Caesar salad without croutons and dressing (220cals)

indian summary

- onion bhaji (180cals)
  swap for popadom (30cals)
- chicken masala (550cals)
  swap for chicken tikka (250cals)
- Lamb rogan josh (500cals)
  swap for vegetable balti (300cals)
- Pilau rice (180cals)
  swap for plain rice (150cals) or naan (100cals)

it's all greek to me

- Doner kebab and salad (700cals)
  swap for Shish kebab with undressed salad (500cals)

shopping for **superfoods**

Some foods are better for you than others, and if you eat more of them, and less of the others, you will enjoy a tasty, nutritious diet, be slimmer, fitter, and live longer. To reap all the benefits, shop for (and eat!) these foods frequently, enjoying a variety from each of the superfood groups.

what superfoods can do

1 supercarbohydrates provide long-lasting energy, B vitamins, and fibre for health protection

2 superfruits can help to protect against diseases and are also packed with vitamins

3 supervegetables are rich in beneficial minerals and fibre

4 superproteins are those that are the leanest, or that contain beneficial fats

5 superfats and oils can help to protect the heart if eaten in moderation

Are some foods superior?

You know by now that for weight control and health you need to eat the bulk of your food as complex carbohydrates, plus lots of fruit and vegetables, limited amounts of meat and its alternatives, limited amounts of milk products, and a very small amount of high-fat and high-sugar foods. And no doubt you are striving to achieve that balance. Good. Some foods from the food groups are, of course, better for you than others. The best thing that you can do is to make a habit of regularly eating the most nutritionally beneficial foods.

superfood maths

$$\text{foods rich in nutrients} + \text{low in calories} = \text{weight control} + \text{healthier, longer life}$$

Superfood carbohydrates

Choose plenty of wholegrain foods and few made with white four. Opt for foods that are lower in sugar and fat (particularly saturated).

Wholemeal and wholegrain – bread and pasta contain wholegrains that are rich in fibre, vitamins, minerals, and antioxidants.

Brown rice is nutritionally better than white rice because it retains fibre and a range of B vitamins and minerals.

Other wholegrains such as bulghur, couscous, barley, buckwheat, millet, oats, quinoa, and rye are all rich in different types of beneficial fibre, vitamins and minerals, and phytochemicals to keep you healthy and help control weight. You can use these wholegrains as ingredients for salads, casseroles, soups, vegetarian, and ethnic recipes. Or find them in breakfast cereals, breads, and other foods – check the labels.

Superfruits

Regularly choose fruits from each of the different colour groups to ensure that you are getting a variety of nutrients. For an extended list of fruits, see p156.

Bananas are a more nutritious energy pick-you-up than sweets and chocolate, as they are rich in B vitamins, including folates, and minerals such as potassium, which helps to prevent or reduce high blood pressure.

Citrus fruits such as oranges, lemons, and limes are great sources of vitamin C, which is essential for all-round health.

Dark berries and cherries are rich in antioxidants. Blackcurrants are a good source of vitamin C, contain some beta-carotene, vitamin E, and a number of beneficial minerals.

Dark orange fruit such as apricots, peaches, mangoes, papaya, persimmon, carambola (starfruit), and tamarillo are good sources of the antioxidant beta-carotene.

Dried fruit such as apricots, dates, peaches, prunes, and raisins are excellent sources of energy, fibre, potassium, and (in the case of apricots) iron.

Supervegetables

Make sure you eat a wide range of different vegetables with your meals to get the maximum benefits. There is an extended list of vegetables on p156.

Alliums such as garlic, onions, shallots, leeks, spring onions, and chives contain sulphur compounds that may increase cancer resistance. They have also been shown to help lower blood cholesterol levels and reduce blood pressure when eaten in sufficient quantity.

Broccoli contains sulphur compounds and may protect against cancer, particularly of the colon.

Green leafy vegetables, such as cabbage, Brussels sprouts, and kale contain heart-healthy folic acid.

Peppers (red, green, yellow, and orange) are rich in all-round health-boosting vitamin C and the antioxidant beta-carotene.

Pumpkin and other varieties of squash and dark yellow or orange sweet potato, are good sources of the antioxidant beta-carotene.

Tomatoes get their colour from lycopene, a carotenoid in their skin that may protect against heart disease and certain cancers. Cook them to get maximum benefit or enjoy them in sauces.

Can't I just take a pill?
Taking vitamin and mineral supplements may seem like a short cut to benefiting from the nutrients in fruit, vegetables, and other foods. But vitamins and minerals work in conjunction with the fibre and phytochemicals in food to boost vitality and provide protection. It is probably the combination of all these factors that reduces the risk of cancer and heart disease. So, eat the right balance of healthy foods for optimum health – but you can boost your vitamins and minerals if you need to. Ask your doctor for advice.

Superproteins

For the best weight control, choose the leanest, most nutritious protein sources wherever possible. Eat a portion of fish at least twice a week in place of meat.

Fish is an excellent source of protein. White fish is low in fat and oily fish contains omega-3 fish oils that help to protect against heart attack.

Lean red meat is far more nutritious than products such as sausages, pies, pâté, salami, and processed meats, which are also higher in unhealthier saturated fat.

Nuts are rich in heart-protective omega-3 fatty acids (walnuts) and unsaturated fat (almonds, peanuts, macadamia), as well as heart-healthy and, probably, cancer-protective selenium (Brazils).

Poultry such as chicken and turkey, has a high percentage of healthier unsaturated fat compared to unhealthier saturated fat.

Beans and pulses including lentils, chickpeas, and soya, are a virtually fat-free source of protein, rich in soluble fibre that helps to lower cholesterol.

Seeds such as sunflower, pumpkin, linseed, and sesame, are rich in protective omega-3 oils, beneficial plant hormones, and vitamin E.

Superfats and oils

You need to cut back on fat for weight control, but make sure the fat you do eat is the right type of fat to prevent health problems. Keep superfats part of a balanced diet.

Avocados contain healthier monounsaturated oil, as well as antioxidant-boosting vitamin E.

Oily fish such as sardines and mackerel contain beneficial omega-3 fatty acids.

Nuts such as almonds, Brazil nuts, and walnuts contain both unsaturated omega-3 oils and monounsaturated fatty acids.

Vegetable oils such as extra-virgin olive oil, sunflower oil, and walnut oil contain heart-healthy polyunsaturated and monounsaturated fats.

Should I go organic?
Organic produce (grown without chemical pesticides and non-organic fertilizers) contain more vitamins and minerals than non-organic foods. Great! Going organic is, however, often the more expensive option, which can be off-putting. Eating insufficient quantities of fruit and vegetables is far more harmful than hazards from the pesticide residues on non-organic foods. If budget is an issue, just buy non-organic.

fish matters

Try to eat fish at least twice a week in place of meat, using oily fish such as salmon, tuna, mackerel, or herring on at least one occasion. The omega-3 fatty acids contained in oily fish have many health benefits including protection against heart disease.

Canned oily fish such as sardines, pilchards, and herring are inexpensive and nutritious and are an excellent source of calcium because of their edible soft bones. Fish canned in tomato sauce is lower in calories than fish canned in oil.

The great thing about fish is that it is so versatile there are so many different ways of preparing, cooking, and presenting fish, so that it is always interesting and delicious.

Low-fat chips
Low-fat home-made oven chips are only 80 calories per portion compared to normal chips at 350 calories. Preheat the oven to 220°C (Gas 7). Peel 700g (1lb 9oz) potatoes and cut into thick chips. Plunge into a saucepan containing about 1 litre (1¾ pints) boiling stock and cook for up to 5 minutes until tender. Drain and allow to cool slightly. Put 2 tbsp vegetable oil in a large polythene food bag or box and carefully "toss" the chips in the fat. Transfer to a non-stick baking tray and bake for 10–15 minutes, turning once or twice, until golden and crisp. Sprinkle with paprika (not salt).

It's all in the cooking

There are many simple, tasty, and healthy cooking methods that you can use for fish. Whether you microwave, poach, grill, barbecue, braise, or bake (the healthiest cooking options), you can add lemon, herbs, and spices – instead of fat. Always go for healthy cooking methods and reap the weight-loss rewards!

Fish and chips?

A great British fast food, but high in fat and calories – it's the frying that does it! Eat this meal very occasionally and, at home, grill fish instead of battering and serve with low-fat chips (see left).

Grilled and barbecued

Baste white fish with lemon juice and just turn frequently during cooking (no need to add fat). Oily fish, such as trout, does not need basting, but a squeeze of lemon will add flavour.

Poached or baked

Poach delicate white fish, such as plaice fillets, or whole oily fish, such as mackerel, in a light vegetable stock. Bake oily fish steaks such as salmon, or firm white fish steaks, such as cod.

healthier **cooking**

As a rule, steam, bake, boil, poach, grill, dry roast, and microwave foods for optimum health benefits in your cooking. Replace processed ingredients with fresh foods, particularly fruit and vegetables, whenever you can. Family members who "don't like vegetables" might not be so reluctant to eat them if they are part of a prepared dish. "Hide" grated carrot, parsnip, and swede by mixing them into dishes such as shepherd's pie, lasagne, and curry – or include them in pizza topping. Limit your use of salty ingredients, such as bacon, anchovies, and olives.

These may seem like small steps, but over time they will make a big difference to the number of calories you consume and you'll also raise your nutrient intake substantially.

Miss Chiplash says: Try to get into the habit of eating bread without butter or any low-fat spread. Multi-grain and rye breads are delicious with soup, cheese, houmus, or avocado spreads and can provide a well-balanced meal or a healthy snack.

think fresh

Fat tactics

There are many ways of limiting the fat content of your cooking.

- Use the leanest meat you can and remove all visible fat. Choose extra lean sausages or burgers and 5–10 per cent fat mince.

- Avoid hard and saturated fats such as lard, ghee, dripping, block margarine, coconut milk, and creamed coconut. Instead, choose unsaturated vegetable oils, such as sunflower, soya, corn, and olive oil. Use all fats sparingly.

- Skim the fat from casseroles and soups before serving them. If you cook these dishes the day before eating them, you can refrigerate them. This makes the fat rise to the top, so you can skim it off easily.

Small fry

Keep frying to a minimum, and use the smallest amount of added fat. Where a recipe states "sauté", which means fry in a little oil, "sweat" the ingredient instead. Put the ingredient in a non-stick pan and cover it with a lid so that that it can cook in its own juices.

Salt and spice

Use spices and herbs instead of adding salt during cooking. Try ethnic spice and herb mixes. Bay leaves, thyme, and coriander are good with meat; tarragon with poultry; parsley and dill with fish; and basil with tomato sauces. Garlic, ginger, and chillies add plenty of flavour. Be sparing with stock cubes, soy sauce, and other sauces because they are high in salt. Try salt-free or low-sodium versions if you have to use them.

here's a *radical thought!*

Stop sprinkling sugar onto breakfast cereal. If you find it difficult, gradually cut down on the amount you add until you wean yourself off. You could replace sugar with a powdered artificial sweetener, but neither will change your underlying tastes and habits.

preserving vitamins and minerals

- Prepare vegetables as close to the cooking or eating time as possible and avoid soaking them in water, to reduce loss of vitamins
- Scrub rather than peel carrots, parsnips, and potatoes. Many health-giving nutrients lie just under the skin

- Don't chop fruit or vegetables too small. Exposing surfaces to the air causes nutrient loss
- Dress cut vegetables and fruit in lemon juice to minimize loss of vitamin C
- Add vegetables to boiling water to reduce the cooking time. Steam when possible

Lower-fat roasting
Place meat on a trivet in a roasting pan so that the fat drains away as the meat cooks. To roast poultry, start it off upside down on a trivet in a roasting pan. This will allow the fat and juices to moisten the drier breast meat as it cooks. Turn the bird for the final half of cooking time to brown.

good habits
start young

Giving children a taste for **healthy food** gives them an **advantage**. Too much high-fat, high-sugar, and high-salt food, along with not being active enough, can result in weight problems. By eating well with your children and finding fun ways to **get active** on a regular basis, you can successfully prevent or tackle weight problems, and enjoy a healthy, happy family life.

the **family approach**

While doctors dither about definitions of obesity and excess weight, parents need to take action on their children's weight. If your child is overweight and your doctor has ruled out any underlying medical cause, don't put him or her on a diet. Because children are still growing, most of them do not need to "lose weight". Instead, their weight gain has to be contained, so that they can "grow into" their weight.

Coping successfully with childhood overweight is about the whole family learning to eat more healthily and become more physically active. Encouraging active play, walking to school, and less time spent playing computer games and watching TV can all help.

Great gains
Reward positive changes in your child's behaviour. If he or she cuts down on sweets, for example, replace them with non-food treats such as stationery, books, or puzzles and games. If your child increases the amount of physical activity that he or she does in a week, buy a gift of an item of clothing suitable for walking or a colourful new cycle helmet, or knee pads to wear when rollerskating or blading.

together

Do it together

If you adjust what your child eats, it is likely that the whole family will eat fewer calories. Cook meals at home as much as possible, so that you are in control of what your child is eating. Replace high-fat fast foods or convenience foods, and fizzy soft drinks, with food choices from the food pyramid (see p92) or the food plate (see p26) and you will soon be eating foods with a lower calorie content and a higher nutrient content. This is excellent for all-round health.

Slowly but surely

Gradual weight loss over time is far healthier than "going on a diet". Slimming diets send the wrong messages to children and can lead to a long-term cycle of dieting, followed by weight gain, resulting in more weight gain as an adult.

Don't be cruel

Your child doesn't have to give up his or her favourite fast foods completely, just encourage him or her to eat them less frequently. If you veto high-fat foods entirely, you might find that your child sneaks out to eat them in secret, building up an unhealthy emotional association with some foods. Try to serve takeaways and convenience foods at home in a healthier way. For simple, tasty ways to make takeaways and convenience foods healthier, see pp64–67.

Use energy to gain energy

By becoming more active, children will burn more calories, which is a quicker and healthier way to control weight than by cutting down on nutritious food. Taking more exercise will also make your child feel more energetic.

Our Fitness Expert says: When you are watching TV as a family, all get up when the advertisements come on and do some activity. Rush off for a run around the garden, walk or run up and down the stairs, do some press-ups, or jump on the exercise bicycle. If the ad breaks are 2 or 3 minutes each, you can add quite a lot of physical activity to your evening. No stairs? Do knee lifts or walk or jog on the spot.

encouraging a healthy lifestyle

- Tackle weight loss as a family, so that your child does not feel singled out
- Change ingredient choices and cooking methods instead of putting your child "on a diet"
- Don't ban high-fat, high-sugar, and high-salt treats – but make your child cut down
- Encourage positive changes by rewarding and praising your child
- Make activity a priority. Set an example by making exercise part of your life, so your child gets used to walking, jogging, or enjoying games as a family

recognizing **child obesity**

We are so used to seeing overweight children that we are beginning to regard overweight as normal. Studies show that the majority of parents of children of primary school age shown drawings of children ranging from underweight to overweight (similar to those shown below) are unable to accurately identify children who are overweight. But what can we do about it? Recognizing and tackling childhood obesity is the responsibility of both parents and schools. To check your child's weight see the boy and girl growth charts (pp152–153).

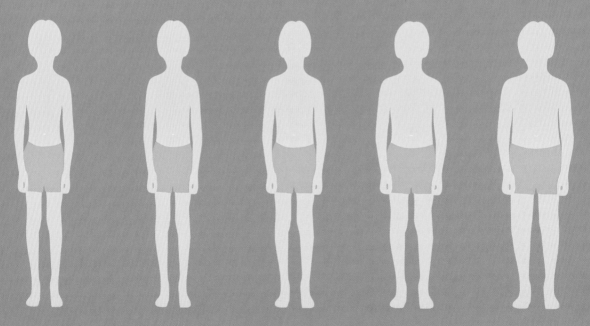

Very underweight
Would benefit from a more nutritious diet

Slightly underweight
Faces no serious health problems at present

Normal weight
The healthy body shape for a child

Slightly overweight
May need to look at diet and exercise

Overweight
May need to speak to a doctor

here's a *radical thought!*

Help your child to understand what's good and what's not, by taking him or her to the supermarket and getting him or her to compare the sugar content of breakfast cereals. The aim is to find a tasty one that contains as little sugar as possible: 10g per 100g is a lot of sugar, 2g per 100g is a little.

Bad break-time habits
Suggest a fruit-only rule for school break times. Send your child into school with a bottle of water. Thirst can be misread for hunger, encouraging overeating. Water is always preferable to fizzy drinks from the school's vending machine.

School of thought
Ask the school to send you a lunch menu to help you balance your child's diet. And does the school encourage active playtimes? Raising funds for climbing frames in school playgrounds is one way parents can help.

feeding **babies**

For the first six months of a baby's life, breast milk provides all the nutrients a baby needs. The recent change of recommendation from weaning at four months to six months may leave some mothers concerned. A baby's digestive system can cope with weaning at four months, but delaying the process reduces the likelihood of developing food intolerance or allergy.

Breastfeeding is best because it provides a baby with perfectly balanced food that changes to meet a baby's needs during the first few months of life. It also provides immunity. Many people think that infant formula is as good as breast milk. It is not – it lacks the antibodies that provide immunity and it doesn't protect against high blood pressure and heart disease in later life.

Home-made or bought?
Whether you have the time and facilities to prepare hygienic food will influence the type of baby food you choose. Home-made food can be more economical food and gives you control over the ingredients. It helps your baby to become used to real foods and gives you the chance to introduce a wider range of foods, which is important in establishing a varied, healthy diet both for childhood and life. It also means you can avoid using non-nutritious fillers such as refined starches, sugar, and additives.

start right

Weaning ways

Introducing food too early could damage your baby's immature gut, kidneys, and liver. Never put foods in a bottle or into expressed breast milk or formula milk as a "taster". Wean your baby at his or her own pace and allow him or her plenty of time to become familiar with different tastes and textures. Always stay with your baby during feeding, because of the risk of choking. Don't force your baby to eat – he or she knows when he or she is full. If hunger and satiation cues are overridden, a baby is more at risk of excessive weight gain.

Getting started

Offer your baby one food at a time before or after a milk feed. Never add salt or sugar to food, even if it tastes bland to you. Start with purées of cooked apple, pear, sweet potato, parsnip, carrot, squash, broccoli, courgette, cauliflower, or swede. You don't need to cook avocado, banana, papaya, and peaches before puréeing. Introduce baby rice as your baby's first cereal, because it is free from gluten, a protein found in wheat, oats, barley, and rye, which can trigger allergy if introduced too early. Keep feeding time relaxed.

Drink it in

During weaning, babies start to need additional drinks to breastfeeds, especially in hot weather. The best drink for babies is cooled, boiled water. Offer drinks (other than breast milk) from a cup or trainer beaker with a spout or a spoon for smaller babies. Don't offer drinks other than milk from a bottle. as this could lead to tooth decay. Fruit squash and drinks are unsuitable for babies because some contain high quantities of sugar or artificial sweeteners.

healthy weaning quantities per day

	6 months*	9 months	12 months
Milk	Cow's milk to mix solids or in yoghurt	5–600ml breast milk; cow's milk (left); hard cheese	5–600ml breast milk; cow's milk (left); hard cheese
Starchy	Rice cereal with milk; mashed starchy vegetables	2–3 servings Wholemeal bread and cereal	3–4 servings Normal texture starchy foods
Fruit and vegetables	Soft-cooked, puréed vegetables and fruit	2 servings Soft fruit and soft vegetables	3–4 servings Lightly cooked or raw; orange juice
Meat and alternatives	Soft-cooked puréed meat or pulses	1 serving Soft or puréed meat or pulses	1 serving meat or milk protein or 2 vegetable protein

*Start with a teaspoonful to taste and increase as necessary

feeding **toddlers**

By the time babies have become toddlers, between one year and 18 months, they should be eating a balanced diet and enjoying a wide variety of foods. They may still be having an early morning breast milk drink and probably going back to sleep before breakfast. Now is a good time to establish the three-meals-a-day pattern, without too many snacks. Keep portions small to begin with and match the consistency of food to your toddler's needs.

age one to two

breakfasts
cereal or toast, porridge, mini muffin, fresh fruit, yoghurt

lunch
soup and bread, or a soft cheese sandwich or bagel spread with soft cheese and stewed fruit. Puddings can include yoghurt and custard with fruit, or fromage frais

dinner
chicken casserole, meat and vegetables, pasta with vegetable soup, or omelette or noodles

bedtime
a bedtime breastfeed can stave off any late-night hunger and keep your child satisfied for the night

age two to three

milk switch
if you are confident your child is having enough nutritious calories, switch to semi-skimmed milk between now and age 5, then to skimmed

portion pointers
stick to 4 portions of carbohydrates (that's starchy foods, not sugary foods) and fruit and vegetables per day and 1 portion of protein

joining in
by this age, toddlers should have a well established 3-meal-a-day eating pattern and be joining family meals

Avoid shopping tantrums

Television advertising ensures that toddlers recognize biscuits, crisps, sweets, sugary breakfast cereals, and fast foods and encourages them to "pester", so expect demands as you shop. Be prepared to politely refuse! If you give your child food to "keep him or her quiet" as he or she sits in the shopping trolley, start as you mean to go on by making it a nutritious snack – fruit pieces, a sandwich, a plain bun, or a mini rice cake. Let your child help to choose fresh fruit and vegetables and put them in a bag. When your toddler is older, ask him or her to collect items (as long as you can keep an eye on him or her) to keep activity a priority.

keeping toddlers happy

- Don't let your toddler fill up on drinks

- Stick to a pattern of regular meal times

- Involve your toddler in food preparation and shopping

- "Hide" vegetables in pasta sauces, pizza toppings, casseroles, and soups

- Serve raw vegetable sticks (carrot, cucumber, pepper, tomato, and celery) as "finger food" for your toddler to handle and enjoy

Dealing with picky eaters

Even the baby who ate up all his or her vegetables might become picky as a toddler. This is common, and is associated with learning to make choices – and learning what bothers parents! The answer is to introduce a simple rule – if your child eats no vegetables, there will be no pudding or treats. For your toddler to establish good eating habits, you as a parent have to be consistent – and, at the same time, avoid making an issue of food. Teaching children healthy eating – and exercise – habits is a great gift. Children need to learn to accept certain "givens" about how many "treats" they are allowed and when. There is no need for temper tantrums or arguments, it can all be done amicably – especially if you stay relaxed and are always calm and consistent in your approach.

it's all about **attitude**

Many children and teenagers have unhealthy eating patterns and an aversion to activity that put their adult health at risk – and affect their ability to learn. As parents, we can help children to grow up with a healthy attitude towards food and exercise.

clever moves

1 make time for your child to have **breakfast**, even if it means he or she goes to bed earlier

2 send your child to school with **a piece of fruit** as a daily snack

3 discourage **meals in front of the TV** – eat around a table (as a family, if possible)

4 **limit fast foods** to occasional treats, but don't associate them with "rewards"

5 **set a daily limit** on time spent watching TV and encourage your child to be active instead

The right healthy balance

For younger children in particular, timing is crucial. Leaving meal times until they are overtired or too hungry will result in them eating very little, refusing food, or wanting snacks between meals. Fruit juice or any sweet foods should be eaten at meal times (rather than as snacks) in order to protect teeth from decay.

Cut it out
Keep a picture of the children's food pyramid (p92) pinned up in the kitchen or stuck to the fridge so that your child will be reminded of healthy eating every time he or she eats at home.

instilling a healthy attitude

- Try not to reward your child with food because this can lead to children (and, later, adults) turning to food for comfort

- Stay objective about food, so that meals times are not emotionally charged

- Avoid self-loathing talk in front of your child, such as complaining that you are fat and having a negative attitude towards your body – or, worse, towards your child's body

Which type are you?

Mothers can divide into two types: the "eat all on your plate" type or the type that instils a dieting habit very early on. The outcome later in life for children is generally that the ones that have been made to clear their plates (and have fewer snacks between meals) turn out not to have a weight problem. "Clearing the plate", should only apply to sensible portions, however, and don't force your child to eat when he or she is not hungry or genuinely dislikes a food. Strike a balance and serve meals with sensible portions of healthy foods.

Lead by example

As a child grows up, he or she absorbs food "beliefs" and habits at home and in the wider community, from TV and peers. Eat healthy, balanced meals with your child and establish regular meal times and eating habits.

portion-distortion challenge

We seem to have forgotten how much we should be eating every day. As meal sizes have grown, so have our bellies. It's time to find out exactly how much you should be eating, weigh out the portions, and serve up. It could be a lot less (but a lot healthier) than you think!

get children **more active**

Good habits are formed early in life, yet some children under six are watching 3–6 hours of television a day, one third of children have televisions in their bedrooms, and many have very little active play at home or at school.

gizmos to get them moving

1 a **skipping rope** with a book of all the slick moves they can learn, such as pretzels and crossovers

2 a **hula hoop** –weighted ones work off abdominal fat quicker than standard ones

3 a **table tennis set** with net, bats, and ball is a great indoor way to get moving

4 **bean bags** and soft balls are good for throwing and catching indoors or out – or for juggling

5 a **soft bat and soft ball** for indoors or a rounders bat and ball for the garden or park

Early birds

Obesity has increased among pre-school children, so try to interest your child in activity early on to prevent problems. You might even form a group of like-minded parents for toddler "strolling" or find a yoga or exercise teacher who specializes in classes for pre-schoolers.

Playing it safe

Check with your local council to see if it has taken up a government scheme to reintroduce park keepers (now called "play rangers") to prevent difficulties for children using parks and open spaces. Or organize a rota of after-school or holiday supervision by parents.

Adult attitude problem

Don't be a killjoy if children are playing football in the park, street, or back alley – let them play, don't tell them off. Active play contributes to children's social and psychological welfare – and stops them becoming overweight. You need to encourage rather than discourage activity.

opportunities for all ages

- Baby and toddler swimming lessons, toddler aerobics, and toddler gym and circuit classes are widely available at leisure and sports centres

- Cycling proficiency certificate courses will help older children become safe cyclists and enable them to take more activity

- After-school clubs for team games, such as rugby, and activities may be available at school or at leisure centres

- Martial arts are a good discipline, build strength, and have the benefit of self-defence (often appealing to older girls – but the younger the better!)

Be a sport

Watching television, videos, and playing computer games are the main leisure activities of the majority of children. Only one in four 5–16 year olds in England regularly plays sport, and many, especially girls, don't exercise and have a negative attitude to activity. Your child needs to take one hour of moderate activity daily, so a great way of doing that is part of a team. Practice sessions with the team and alone soon add up.

Holiday camps

Summer holiday sports camps can be a source of fun as well as activity for children of all ages. Both local authorities and independent organizations use qualified teachers and sports students for programmes of structured sports and games. Many offer sports that your child may not have tried before, such as climbing or canoeing, and they also offer popular activities such as trampolining, dance, or drama.

Our Fitness Expert says: Get your child to colour in a chart that logs his or her hours of active play during the week. He or she can draw a circle and colour in 15-minute segments of activity time to make up an hour a day.

teenagers **on the move**

For most teenagers, exercise is off limits. Making it an integral part of their life is more difficult than when you start earlier with younger children. Choosing the right activities is even more important when you are trying to motivate and excite teenagers as they are all too quick to declare an activity "borrrringgg!".

getting teens going

1 identify if your teenager is a **team player** or if he or she is more likely to exercise **alone**

2 then suggest your teenager **enrols in a team** or gets equipped for **jogging or skateboarding**

3 try to get him or her interested in something different, such as a school **orienteering** programme

4 invest in a **playstation dance mat** or **exercise bike** for home-based action

5 seek out a local **athletics group** – your teenager may enjoy the long jump or javelin

Sedentary sports fans

For a nation that is supposed to be "sports mad" (especially boys and football), there are too few actually doing it – most just sit and watch. It's time for your teenager to get up off the sofa, or out of the stands, and get physical. See if he or she can emulate a favourite sports personality by getting kitted out and fitted out for action!

Benefits now

Taking more physical activity helps to control weight and reduce body fat, stress, and anxiety. It also makes the brain function faster. So active adolescents will not only be slimmer, more toned, and more attractive, but they could also be more academically successful. If they start moving more, they can reap the benefits at exam time.

Moody blues

Teenagers can be very moody and can experience mild depression for a variety of reasons. Taking part in moderate and vigorous physical activity can noticeably improve your teenager's emotional state and general wellbeing. Encourage your teenager to be more active as a means of tackling the blues and chasing teen troubles away.

Benefits in the future

Your teenager may have more pressing concerns than his or her future health, but the effort he or she puts in now will pay off in years to come. Being active and eating well now means a lower risk of heart attack, stroke, and osteoporosis in later years. Bone density peaks in the late teens and is dependent on high-impact activity.

Shop so you don't drop
Most women walk nearly 3 miles when they go shopping for something specific (other than the groceries), which they do about once a month, clocking up an estimated 133 miles a year. Sounds like a suitable activity for teenage girls...

pushing the right buttons

- Let them make music – a drum kit may be the answer (preferably a kit with silent rubber drums and headphones) to your teen's activity needs

- Appeal to vanity – if your teenager makes the connection between better body shape and physical activity, he or she might be more motivated

- Buy a dog – or borrow a neighbour's, giving your teenager the responsibility of taking it for walks (and runs)

- Watch a video – but make it a yoga or a fitness video to encourage activity in the "living" room rather than lounging in the "sitting" room

Wrestling with the future
Teenage boys 14–18 years old who take up wrestling have far more efficient immune systems than their sedentary peers. In general, exercise boosts immunity so they won't catch cold so frequently.

children's **food pyramid**

The best way to reinforce good eating habits is to eat together as a family as often as possible. If your child sees you eating and enjoying a balance of nutritious foods, he or she will be more likely to want to eat healthy foods, too.

1 children **consistently** offered a balanced diet early in life develop good eating habits

2 **use the food pyramid** to make easy work of healthy eating for children

3 **up to age five**, portion (or serving) sizes should be around two thirds of adult size

4 **after age five**, use the adult portion guide (see pp26–27 and pp32–35)

5 **to control weight**, children must be physically active as well as eating healthily

The pyramid points the way

• Bread, potatoes, pasta, rice, porridge, breakfast cereal, and other cereals are important for energy, vitamins and minerals, and fibre – encourage a variety of wholegrain starchy (or grain) foods such as wholemeal bread and brown rice.

• Encourage children to eat five fruits and vegetables a day and offer a wide a variety of colours, such as dark green leafy, deep orange and yellow, and red fruits and berries. Give these as snacks instead of sweets and crisps.

• Meat, fish, eggs, lentils, pasta, and nuts (if your child is not allergic) are important for protein and for minerals such as iron.

• Milk is important for most young children. Serve full-fat milk up to the age of two, then you can switch to semi-skimmed milk (if your child has a nutritious diet). You can change to skimmed after the age of five.

• Fatty and sugary foods such as cakes, sweets, and fizzy drinks form the tip of the pyramid and should be eaten in small quantities.

weight control plan **for children**

Weight control in children is about eating healthily and learning to choose sensible portions of nutritious food – it is not about dieting. Enjoying a variety of foods is important, so introduce your child to a variety of foods from the main food groups.

children's calorie needs

1 **4–6 years** – boys require 1,715 calories a day, and girls require 1,545

2 **7–10 years** – boys require 1,970 calories a day, and girls require 1,740

3 **11–14 years** – boys require 2220 calories a day, and girls require 1,845

4 **15–18 years** – boys require 2,755 calories a day, and girls require 2,110

5 **over 18** – boys require 2,550 calories a day, and girls require 1,940 calories

Eat for your age

Controlling children's weight is best achieved by eating the right amount for their age, being active, and "growing into" any excess weight. But if your doctor advises that a reduction in calories could be helpful, a 1600 calorie plan is a good template for healthy eating – it suits children aged 7–14. For a younger child, gradually reduce his or her portion intake to match the children's food pyramid (see p92). An older child could use the plans on pp32–35.

(see p92)

on pp32–35.

Active children
If your child is very active, he or she may need to eat more than the guidelines suggest, but increase portions of complex (starchy) carbohydrates rather than simple (sugary) carbohydrates. Very sporty adolescents may "get away with" an extra sugary treat now and again – but not too often!

children's eating plan

1600 calorie menu

breakfast

1 glass fruit juice
1 wholegrain cereal with milk from allowance
1 slice wholemeal bread
1 tsp polyunsaturated spread

lunch

2–3 tbsp cooked wholemeal pasta
3 tbsp tomato or vegetable pasta sauce
1 apple
1 slice malt loaf (no spread)

evening

60–90g (2–3oz) grilled or poached salmon or poultry
60–90g (2–3oz) cooked noodles, peas, and carrots
1 satsuma or 1 fruit yoghurt

plus…

0.5 litres (1 pint) skimmed or semi-skimmed milk
1 piece of fruit
Unlimited raw or cooked vegetables (except potatoes)

Kids and fizz

Fizzy drinks contribute to childhood obesity. One can could add as much as 15 teaspoonfuls of sugar to your child's daily diet. That's 10 per cent of your child's total calorie intake, and over time that adds up to a lot of weight gain. Cut the fizz and you'll cut the calories – and save your child's teeth!

minor-chef challenge

It's time to give the grown-ups the day off and let the minor chefs loose in the kitchen. Cooking healthy, nutritious food can be so simple, it's child's play, using oh-so-easy recipes for soups, salads, fish, and pasta dishes – all the nation's favourites! Relax and watch the kids cook up a culinary storm!

lunchboxes packed with health

Children's lunchbox surveys show that most provide more fat, sugar, and salt than is recommended. Lifting the lid reveals a white bread sandwich, crisps, a biscuit or chocolate bar, and a full-fat yoghurt or dessert. Fewer than half of children's lunchboxes contain a portion of fruit, and many contain fizzy drinks. All these foods are contributing to expanding waistlines and weight problems. Here are tips for how to prepare the ideal lunchbox:

- For food safety, use an insulated bag or a box with an ice pack

- Include at least 1 food from each food group

- Pack no more than 1 small treat a day, such as a fun-size chocolate bar

- Avoid serving a whole bag of crisps – put a few in a small sealable tub

- Steer clear of nuts (other children may have allergies)

- Include a small bottle or flask of water every day

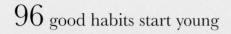

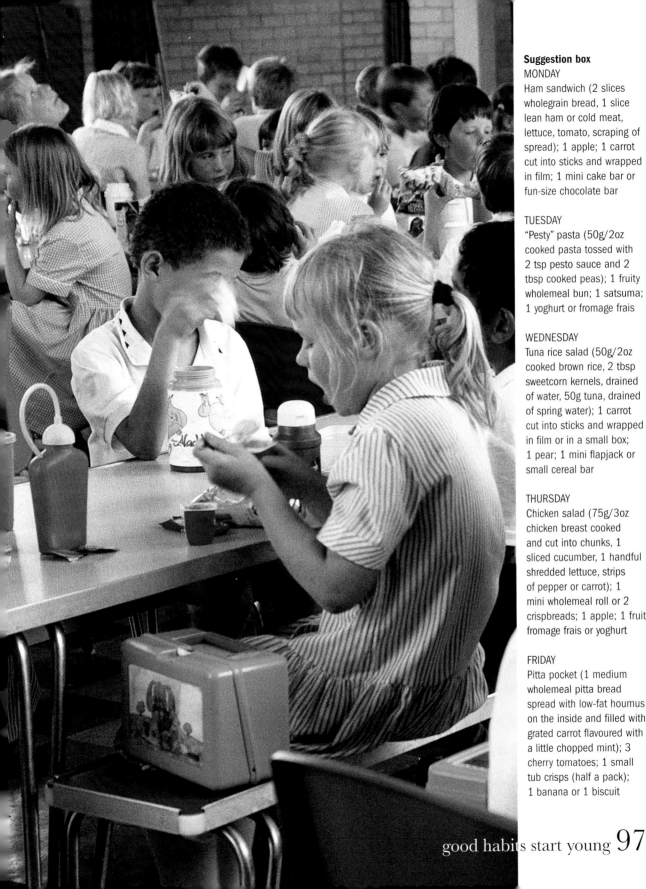

MONDAY
Ham sandwich (2 slices
wholegrain bread, 1 slice
lean ham or cold meat,
lettuce, tomato, scraping of
spread); 1 apple; 1 carrot
cut into sticks and wrapped
in film; 1 mini cake bar or
fun-size chocolate bar

TUESDAY
"Pesty" pasta (50g/2oz
cooked pasta tossed with
2 tsp pesto sauce and 2
tbsp cooked peas); 1 fruity
wholemeal bun; 1 satsuma;
1 yoghurt or fromage frais

WEDNESDAY
Tuna rice salad (50g/2oz
cooked brown rice, 2 tbsp
sweetcorn kernels, drained
of water, 50g tuna, drained
of spring water); 1 carrot
cut into sticks and wrapped
in film or in a small box;
1 pear; 1 mini flapjack or
small cereal bar

THURSDAY
Chicken salad (75g/3oz
chicken breast cooked
and cut into chunks, 1
sliced cucumber, 1 handful
shredded lettuce, strips
of pepper or carrot); 1
mini wholemeal roll or 2
crispbreads; 1 apple; 1 fruit
fromage frais or yoghurt

FRIDAY
Pitta pocket (1 medium
wholemeal pitta bread
spread with low-fat houmus
on the inside and filled with
grated carrot flavoured with
a little chopped mint); 3
cherry tomatoes; 1 small
tub crisps (half a pack);
1 banana or 1 biscuit

easy food **for children**

Children like and deserve tasty food, but that doesn't mean they need expensive "children's foods" from supermarkets and fast-food chains. As a parent, you will do your child a big favour if you help him or her to develop a taste for simpler lower-fat and lower-salt foods.

Learning to like the taste of "real" food and learning some basic food, nutrition, and cookery preparation skills is the aim. This will equip children to make healthier choices for their future. However, while they are still young, they are dependent on parents and school to feed them well. With busy lives, it's important to have some quick and easy foods that will be acceptable to children to eat – not boring, occasionally original, and including a few treats … so here goes. Wash your hands, sit up at the table, and tuck in.

Improving fast-food favourites

Fish and chips Choose oven-baked (lower-fat) fish in batter and chips. Serve smaller portions of fish and chips and accompany with peas and carrots.

Burger Choose leaner versions and serve with salad in the bun, with no mayonnaise or added cheese. Serve extra vegetables on the side.

Pizza Choose lower-fat pizzas such as cheese and tomato and serve strips of lean meat alongside, rather than serving higher-fat pepperoni pizza. Cut into small slices and serve only 1–3 slices with plenty of vegetables.

yum, yum

From the freezer

Keep peas, carrots, broccoli, broad beans, spinach, green beans, and vegetable mixtures in the freezer ready for use. Other useful standbys are sliced wholegrain bread (for speedy sandwiches and toast), pancakes, wholemeal scones, fishcakes, small pieces (fillets or steaks) of salmon, lean burgers, chicken thighs, legs, or breasts, prawns, fish fingers, skimmed milk, and soup. Always serve main meals with two types of vegetables – for example, grilled chicken or salmon with peas and carrots.

From the cupboard

Stock up with cans of sweetcorn (in water), tuna and salmon (in water), sardines, kidney (and other) beans, and tomatoes for cooking sauces. Keep tinned tomatoes ready to be whipped up into pasta sauces or pizza topping. Line up jars of herbs for flavouring instead of salt. Fill the cupboard with packets of breakfast cereal and porridge oats. Keep bags of dried fruit (apricots, raisins, and prunes) at the ready for sprinkling on top. Cereal is great for a snack – stow away some longlife milk for emergencies!

Quick meal ideas

- Toasted sandwiches with salad on the side and chopped raw vegetables.
- Scrambled eggs on wholemeal toast.
- Couscous with ratatouille.
- Stir fried vegetables with thin chunks or strips of fresh salmon.
- Lamb kebabs (neck fillet of lamb) – chunks of lamb, cherry tomatoes, courgette slices, slices of red/green pepper, onion chunks (optional). Cook under the grill or on a BBQ
- Fishcakes (home-made from poached fish and mashed or roughly crushed cooked potato, optional chopped herbs). Served with peas and courgettes.

children's meal swaps

6 year old's dream tea:

Jam or chocolate spread sandwich (sliced white bread), chocolate bar, crisps, and high-sugar fruit drink

better choices:

- Tuna and soft cheese sandwich (wholemeal bread, or half white and half brown, 1 slice of each), a banana, and fruit juice
- Pasta shapes tossed with shredded lean meat or poultry, fruit, a digestive biscuit, and water
- Smoked mackerel dip (fish mashed with soft cheese or natural yoghurt), vegetable sticks and mini rice cake(s) for dipping, and apple juice

11 year old's dream tea:

Cheese sandwich (sliced white bread), crisps, chocolate bar, and a can of fizzy drink

better choices:

- Mashed sardine sandwiches, natural yoghurt with crunchy oat cereal stirred in, apricots or plums, and fruit juice
- Cheese and coleslaw salad (white cabbage, carrots, apple, celery, dried dates, grated cheddar in yoghurt or mayonnaise), savoury scone, apple or pear, and fruit juice
- Grilled lean sausage and salad sandwich, yoghurt, slice of malt loaf, and milk or yoghurt drink

helping teenagers **be healthy**

Teenagers are very body conscious but their self-awareness does not always mean they are carefully eating a balanced diet and taking exercise to look good. The most likely connection between their appearance and health habits is a common misconception that chocolate gives them spots and a fanaticism for dieting among teenage girls.

For many parents of teenagers, concerns about healthy eating and weight control may seem less important than their children's experimentation with smoking and drinking (and possibly recreational drugs). However, there are many practical things parents can do to help teenagers achieve a healthy balance.

"There's nothing to eat!"

When your teenager looks in the fridge and says "there's nothing to eat" (meaning there are no convenience or fast foods), encourage him or her to feel at home in the kitchen and cook something. You could cook with your child, choosing healthy staple foods and teaching the basics: pasta, stir frying, grilling meat and fish, preparing vegetables, baking potatoes, creating a salad, making sandwiches, boiling an egg, making an omelette, or a smoothie. Your teenager may even find that he or she has a talent for culinary creations and may wish to cook for the family – bliss!

teenage tricep dips

While your teenager is watching TV or a DVD, encourage him or her to do this armchair arm-toning exercise

- Sit on the edge of a chair with your hands immediately either side of your bottom and the heel of your hands to the edge of the chair

- Move your bottom forwards just enough to clear the seat. Bend at the elbow and lower your bottom directly towards the floor – count to 4 as you descend

- When you reach the limit of the range of movement in your shoulder, press the heel of your hands into the chair to push back up to the point just before your elbows lock. Count to 2 and repeat

Skinny now, fat later?

If your teenager has become so body conscious that he or she has started to diet or skip meals in order to slim down, it's time for a bit of body education. Explain that while cutting down dramatically on food intake may seem to be effective for weight loss, it will in fact lead to weight gain in the long term. That's because dieting means that the body adjusts to existing on fewer calories and once your teenager resumes "normal" eating, he or she will gain weight quickly. So quite apart from losing out on all the beneficial nutrients in good food, your body-conscious teenager could be setting up big weight problems for the future.

Big eaters
Children served larger portions than they need go on to serve themselves larger portions at subsequent meals. Explain to teenagers that food industry "supersizing" from confectionery to burgers and fizzy drinks, is designed to make them eat bigger portions (to increase industry profits) and that the smart thing to do is to stick to sensible portions.

good habits start young 101

teenage issues on a plate

Adolescents are eating too much fat and salt (from fast foods, convenience foods, and takeaways), and too much sugar (sometimes replacing meals with sweets and fizzy drinks). Most teens exist on a diet of white bread, pizza, chips, crisps, biscuits, and chocolate – a recipe for disaster!

make it easy to eat healthily

1 try to make **breakfast, lunch, and dinner** important landmarks in your family day

2 strike a deal so that you eat at least **some meals as a family** on week nights

3 **limit the choice** of unhealthy foods in your fridge and cupboards (and don't be seen eating them yourself!)

4 make **healthy snacks**, such as fresh fruit, low-fat yoghurt, and low-fat cereal bars readily available

5 a **vitamin and mineral supplement** is a good insurance policy for picky teenage eaters and dieters

I know, I know

On the whole, teenagers know what constitutes a healthy diet but they do not put the rules into action when choosing their own food. Yet many feel unhappy because of their weight problems. Improving food available in the home and encouraging family-based physical activity will help.

Do the maths!

Appeal to your teenager's logic by pointing out the following. One kingsize chocolate bar (450cals) requires 1¼ hours of low-impact aerobics to burn off. Those 450 calories could be spent on 1 glass of orange juice, 1 slice of toast with spread and marmalade, and a bowl of cereal with semi-skimmed milk.

No smoke without fags
Trying to get across the idea to teenagers that it is not "cool" to smoke and that eating well and exercising are better ways to a good body image and more self-confidence is a challenge. Try telling young girls that smoking is not the way to control weight! Persuade teenagers that there are far better alternatives to smoking for stress relief, such as exercise.

vegetarian meal swaps

teen's dream veggie meal

Salad sandwich, crisps, chocolate bar, and cola or squash

better choices:

1. Houmus and grated carrot in wholegrain bread roll, fruit fool, flapjack, and a smoothie

2. Wedge of vegetable (such as pea and carrot) tortilla (or slice of cold cooked omelette), bread roll, and an individual summer pudding

3. Salad of crunchy red cabbage, apple, and cashews or peanuts in light dressing, oatmeal cookie, and pitted prunes or other dried fruit snack

Teen bones

About half of adult bone density (bone strength) is laid down during adolescence, so provide plenty of good sources of calcium in the form of low-fat milk products, eggs, wholegrain cereals, sardines (and other canned fish in which the bones are eaten), pulses, nuts, seeds, dark green vegetables, and fortified soya milk products. Adequate calories in a healthy balanced diet (plus exercise) is the key to healthy bone strength and growth.

Too tired to party?

Many teenagers lounge around looking pale and interesting. Could it be iron deficiency? Iron fortified breakfast cereals are useful for vegetarians and to meet increased iron needs when girls start to menstruate. Drinking orange juice with vegetable sources of iron (such as green leafy vegetables, pulses, eggs, dried apricots, and wholemeal bread) also helps absorption. Avoid tea and coffee for 30 minutes after meals to increase absorption.

Miss Chiplash says:
Prevent and eliminate possible food cravings in teenagers by ensuring a balance of food groups at every meal.

in shape for a
lifetime

Whatever your age, it is **never too late** to improve your diet, get fit, and start losing weight if you need to. Even small changes to your day-to-day life make a **big difference**, over time. Whether you're in your 20s or your 70s, there are **specific changes** that you can make to your eating habits and activity levels, to keep you trim as the years go by. Think good health for life and enjoy yourself!

in shape **in your 20s**

The 20s are a time for having fun, travelling, going out, enjoying dating, completing education, and finding your feet in the world of work. All this doesn't leave a lot of time for thinking about weight and health problems, let alone acting on them. But staying in shape can be easy and will give you more energy to do all the things you want to do.

fun ways to stay in shape

1 **cook a healthy, nutritious** meal at least once a week and invite all your friends round for a tasting

2 **carry snacks** such as fruit, dried fruit, and nuts to prevent unhealthy impulse buys!

3 **skate around town** to build muscles in your legs and firm and tone your thighs and bum

4 **cycle to meet your friends** – if it's at the pub, it'll also ensure that you limit your alcohol intake

5 **dance the night away** for some excellent after-hours aerobic exercise

Start being active for life

If you have not already got the exercise habit, start now, because you need to be active throughout life. The 20s is when you reach peak bone mass, so it's important to eat calcium-rich foods (see p103) and exercise. Throughout life there is a constant turnover of minerals in the bones and the danger is that you could have a deficit as large as your student loan if you don't act.

Strengthen bones

The way to slow down the loss of minerals and to strengthen bones is to do regular weight-bearing exercise at either high- or low-impact aerobic levels. If you choose the more aerobic activities such as jogging, running, climbing stairs, and active sports you will also lose weight and improve your heart and lung health for all-round fitness.

here's a
radical thought!

If you do not take up regular physical activity now, you may find getting out of an armchair or the bath will be totally exhausting by the time you are in your late 70s. From your mid-20s your aerobic capacity decreases by about 1 per cent a year. There are immediate benefits too, such as better weight control and a more gorgeous-looking you.

crunch time for tummies

1. Sit forward on your chair so that your knees are over your ankles at a 90-degree angle

2. Sit up tall as though a wire is pulling you up from the top of your head. Suck in your tummy (belly button to spine)

3. Crunch your breast bone downwards and tilt your pelvic bones upwards – in effect, you are doing a seated "crunch" as your spine arches to a "C"

4. Hold the crunch for 30 seconds (but keep breathing) and then relax. Do 3 or 4 an hour

Join the club

If you are trying to lose weight and finding it hard going on your own without the support of family, friends, or colleagues, then joining a reputable slimming club or a club with an online or email "support group" can be a great help. You can use the professional advice of the club's experts in conjunction with activities and exercises that fit well into your life.

Careering out of control

Working on your career may seem more important than working on your weight. But even the busiest student or career person can find time for activity. Find an active way to get from A to B – cycling or skating can be quicker than taking the bus or driving – and always walk up and down stairs at college, work, and at home. You can do tummy crunches (see above) at your desk!

Get out more
When the weather is mild, swap running on the treadmill for running in the park. Running on grass is 10 per cent more difficult than running on a treadmill – it forces you to use more strength, giving tummy muscles a better workout. It will also improve balance and coordination – and you can enjoy the fresh air and the view!

in shape **during pregnancy**

Ideally women should be a healthy weight before pregnancy. Being either underweight or obese increases risks of a low-birth-weight baby who may have future health problems as a consequence.

safe ways to stay in shape

1 tone down any jogging or running that you did before you were pregnant to **power walking**

2 switch from high-impact aerobics to **low-impact aerobics, aqua aerobics, or swimming**

3 reduce any **weight work** to lighter weights with fewer repetitions

4 **after 12 weeks**, avoid any exercises that require you to lie on your back

5 stop doing an exercise **if you feel sick, tired or dizzy** – and don't get so breathless that you can't speak

Your weight gain

Weight gain during pregnancy is about 12.5kg (nearly 2 stone). Most gain starts after the first 12 weeks and should be a steady 400g (just under 1lb) a week. It is made up of the weight of the baby, increased blood and other body fluids, body fat – varying in women between 2kg (4½lb) and 10kg (1½ stone), the placenta that nourishes the baby, and the fluid that surrounds the baby.

Eating for two?

If you put on too much weight during your pregnancy, it'll be harder to get back in shape after your baby is born. You only need to eat an extra 200 calories per day from the 27th week of your pregnancy. These should be healthy, nutritious calories, of course – you can't just eat a couple of chocolate bars and hope for the best! Quality is key.

Top up your folates
Folates are a type of B vitamin found in green leafy vegetables, pulses, and oranges. They are added to fortified breakfast cereals and some other foods as folic acid, a nutrient that reduces the risk of neural tube defects such as spina bifida. If you are planning a pregnancy, take a daily supplement of 400mcg of folic acid. Continue with the tablets for the first 12 weeks of pregnancy. If you are already pregnant, start taking folic acid now.

eating to avoid excess weight gain

staple foods

- Wholegrain cereal foods
- Fruit and vegetables
- Lean protein
- Oily fish
- Low-fat milk products

plus 200 calories

- 1 small piece of fruit cake
- 1 large bowl of cereal with semi-skimmed milk and chopped fruit
- 1 glass of milk or low-sugar shake
- 70g (3oz) houmus with vegetable sticks and a small pitta bread

Fit for pregnancy

During pregnancy, continue – or even begin – to exercise regularly, but at a low to moderate intensity. You need to work at a lower intensity because during pregnancy you have more blood in your body and, therefore, reduced oxygen levels, so aerobic activity becomes more difficult. Consult your doctor before exercising to check that it is safe for you and for your baby.

Reap the benefits

The benefits of exercise during pregnancy are that you will increase your stamina and help to prevent or reduce unpleasant pregnancy-related problems such as constipation and varicose veins. Your increased stamina could help you when it comes to your baby's birth, and afterwards when your normal sleep patterns are disturbed by your baby's night feeds.

here's a
radical thought!

Your centre of gravity shifts as your pregnancy progresses, so you need to be careful about your posture in your everyday activities and, in particular, when you exercise. Do not stand still for long periods – keep moving.

in shape **in your 30–40s**

Whether you are a professional 30-something who is more focused on career than having a family, or one of the growing band of older parents juggling work and family and trying to do or have it all, you still need to address weight and health issues.

reasons to do it now

1 prevent **middle-age spread** (which could be up to 1kg) through diet and exercise

2 now is when muscle loss increases, so make an effort to **stay toned**

3 losing weight now can **help to prevent sleep problems** (children permitting!)

4 **a brisk daily walk** of 30 minutes halves the risk of Type 2 diabetes for "middle-aged" women

5 small fitness improvements now mean **reduced risk of premature death** in men

No time for health

Children at home or a career-orientated lifestyle can make healthy eating and exercise difficult. Take opportunities around work and home life to prepare healthy food and take exercise. Everyday sport is about being active without disrupting your busy life. It means you run up the stairs, jog to the bus stop, or suggest a lunchtime team game with colleagues.

De-stressing

Stress at work and home can take its toll on your mental as well as physical health, leaving you feeling tired. You may be using caffeine to keep going, which (in the form of a full-fat latte) can be fattening. And if you are also drinking alcohol in order to relax after work, or after the children have gone to bed, then this could also contribute to a weight problem.

here's a
radical thought!

Try something completely different as a form of relaxation and exercise – for example, have drumming or singing lessons. The sense of rhythm and the improved breathing techniques help reduce stress and the activities are fun and lively.

healthy ideas for busy people

- Take turns with your partner to go out for an evening walk after the kids have gone to bed

- Have healthy shopping or a "fruit and veg" box home delivered if necessary – it takes minutes to do it online

- Jump on your bike for local errands, such as posting a letter or going to the bank

- Take up a martial art for excellent all-round fitness in middle age – a great alternative to the gym

The bottom line on cellulite

Women – stop obsessing about cellulite. If you read glossy women's magazines, you will know that many gorgeous celebrities have cellulite, too. The best treatment for the dimpled orange-peel effect just under the skin is calorie-burning and muscle-toning exercises. You could cut back on fat and salt, too, as these encourage fluid retention.

fruity-flirty challenge

How many of us eat our 5 portions of fruit and veg a day? Ask your kids to get fruity - "give me 5"! And once the kids are in bed, it's time for the grown-ups' challenge - to get a bit...well... fruity. You can burn loads of calories in an evening of flirting, cuddling, kissing, and more...

in shape **in your 50–60s**

Glamorous celebrities are a great role model to stop you putting your feet up in your 50s and 60s, even if you have retired. Now is no time to throw in the towel when it comes to healthy eating and physical activity. In fact, circumstances may now be easier for health than they have ever been. This could be the time to take advantage and go for it!

no excuse now because

1 you may have **more time** without the day-to-day constraints of work or the routine of childcare

2 you might have the opportunity to take grandchildren on **active days out**

3 you might find you have **more money** to spend on healthy activities and food

4 you may be at home more, so that looking after (and exercising) **a dog**, could work for you

5 you can afford to be a bit **more selfish** and put your health and fitness needs first

No time to pause

For women, changes associated with the menopause increase the risk of osteoporosis and heart disease. Taking enough of the right sort of exercise can help to reduce the risk of these (and other) health problems. Even if you have never exercised before, regular exercise will help to maintain bone density and reduce the risks – exercise can help any mood swings, too.

Men's health

The male menopause may not be medically recognized, but loss of libido, negative moods, lethargy and fatigue, loss of hair, muscle tone, and strength – and weight gain – are all common. Men's symptoms can be helped by activity and a good diet based on sensible portions of low-fat food, fresh fruit and vegetables, wholegrain foods, and essential fatty acids.

plan an active retirement

Do those things you have always dreamed of

- Take the opportunity to travel and see as much of the world as you can
- Buy a motorbike and set out on the high road!
- Learn to fly a kite, a helicopter, a glider, or a plane
- Take a challenge and climb a mountain
- Learn to parachute
- Become a volunteer for an overseas charity
- Don't be restrained by the convention of sitting in an armchair, putting up your feet – get up and stay active!

Wine and women

Wine drinkers often talk about the health benefits of alcohol. The greatest protection against heart disease from alcohol is for menopausal women, however. For women aged 44–74, two units of alcohol a day may offer some protection against heart disease and stroke. For everyone else, know your limits (see pp136–137).

Pool your activities

If aerobics are becoming a bit of a strain because of stiff joints or accumulated injuries, try water workouts. Water offers resistance so that muscles can work harder than on dry land – but without the risk of injury. Even though you are working at a lower intensity, what you lose in aerobic fitness, you gain in potential to burn off more fat.

Salt it out!
About 40 per cent of people aged 50–59, have high blood pressure. Eating less salt helps to reduce blood pressure, so cut down to no more than 1 tsp per day. This includes salt in processed foods and salt added during cooking, as well as at the table. If you eat less than 3g of salt per day, you can lower your blood pressure, reducing the risk of stroke by 22 per cent and of heart attack by 15 per cent.

in shape **in your 70s**

Being as sprightly as you were in your 50s (or sprightlier) is an achievable goal. There's a wide variation in how quickly people "wind down" with age and two people in their 70s are likely to be more dissimilar than two younger people of the same age. Some variability is partly due to your genes, but how fat and how fit you are have a bearing.

staying in shape **safely**

1 **begin** by exercising for 5 minutes, 3 times a day and build it up

2 work within the range of motion that your **joints** allow

3 exercise in **water** to support your body and reduce the impact on your joints

4 concentrate on building **flexibility** and working on **endurance**

5 **don't overdo it** by doing exercise for too long or at too high an intensity

Food and fitness

The nutritional quality of your diet is of utmost importance now because you may have found that your appetite has reduced over the past few years. Choose wisely, including vitamin- and mineral-rich foods. Physical activity will also help to control your weight and improve your fitness, even if you have Type 2 diabetes, heart disease, or high blood pressure (but check with your doctor before you start).

Circulate

Most people regard heart disease as a male problem. The truth is that nearly as many women as men die from heart disease every year in Britain. In addition, about 60 per cent of people over the age of 70 have high blood pressure (a reading of 140/90mmHg). All the more reason to eat lots of fruit and vegetables, of varied colours, exercise regularly and wisely, and reduce your salt intake.

top-to-toe exercises

Neck Hold onto the sides of a chair and sit up tall, facing forward. Relax your shoulders, lengthen your neck, and lower your head to one side so that your ear goes towards your shoulder

Shoulders Raise your shoulders up close to your ears and roll them back, then bring them up and into a forwards roll and finally up and back to the starting position

Spine Put your right hand on your left knee and your left hand behind you so that it is over the edge of the back of a chair. Sit up tall and turn your head to look over your shoulder, rotating your spine and trunk as you look behind you

Hips Stand to the side of a chair, holding the back of the chair with your feet hip-distance apart. Lift one knee slowly to hip height, then lower it again and repeat with the other leg. Do this for 1 minute, so that you slowly march on the spot

Knees Sit up straight towards the front of a chair, with your feet flat on the floor and your knees making a right angle to the floor. With your tummy pulled in tight (belly button to spine), slowly raise one foot off the floor with the foot flexed (toes pointing at the ceiling) and bring it up until your leg is at right angles to the floor. Hold for 2 seconds and repeat with the other foot

Life gains
If you are feeling fed up and are not particularly inspired by the idea of exercise, give it a try because regular physical activity can help you sleep better, give an improved sense of wellbeing, and aid weight control. Losing weight also improves symptoms of arthritis by reducing the strain on inflamed and painful joints.

staying
healthy

Being overweight is a risk factor for a number of medical conditions, such as Type 2 diabetes, high blood pressure, **heart disease**, and certain cancers. If you **commit to change**, however, you can reduce the risks of developing these conditions and **prevent** their onset. Making changes can also help you to **treat** health problems, if you have them, so that you feel healthier and fitter.

weight gain and **disease**

Many diseases are a result of weight problems. As waistlines expand, the number of people with long-term diseases increases. Longer life expectancy means that we have an added incentive to make positive changes to our diet and lifestyle to enjoy an active retirement. Prevent and treat health problems by acting now.

shocking statistics

1 **30,000 premature deaths a year** may be caused by obesity

2 around **1 million cases of Type 2 diabetes** remain undiagnosed in the UK

3 **70,000 new cases of cancer** a year in Europe are attributable to overweight

4 **80,000 cancer cases** a year in the UK are contributed to by diet

5 obesity and diet-induced disease **rival smoking** as one of the major causes of preventable death

Global health burden

Obesity could be the biggest global health burden – a problem that will plague us for the next 30 years. Obesity itself is not recognized by all doctors as a serious disease that can be treated and many doctors do not see weight management as their role. If your doctor can't help, seek help elsewhere (see p160).

18 million sickies

It's estimated that 18 million sick days a year in the UK are attributable to obesity, placing a huge strain on the economy. Don't let yourself get to that stage – tackle your weight issues now to prevent health problems that could affect your professional life. There are always solutions – stay positive.

what can I do?

- Don't panic! The health facts may be shocking, but they are not inevitable. You can take charge of your health
- Take it slowly. If you have a little weight to lose, you will see health benefits quickly. If you have a lot of weight to lose, be patient and keep going
- Get help if you need to. Contact your health authority if you need more support than you are currently getting
- Think positively. You have the power and, if you change your lifestyle, you will have the stamina to do it for you and for your family

Time to waist away

No matter how big you are, losing 10cm (4ins) from around your stomach will reduce your chances of developing weight-related health problems such as Type 2 diabetes or heart disease. If you already have one of these illnesses, your condition will also be improved. So whittle away your waistline and lengthen your lifespan.

General rules

To reduce weight, and disease risk, eat more fruit and vegetables, cut your fat intake (particularly saturated fat), eat less salt, and take about one hour's moderate activity a day. By doing these few things you really can add years to your life and preserve your health for longer. There's never been a better reason to shed the pounds.

Scale of the problem
In 1980 the average British man weighed 73.7kg (11½ stone) and the average British woman weighed 62.6kg (9½ stone). By 2000 that had increased to 81.6kg (12½ stone) and 68.8kg (10½ stone).

preventing **Type 2 diabetes**

Being overweight and having a sedentary lifestyle are the main reasons why a growing number of of people in their 40s or younger have Type 2 diabetes, a condition in which the body cannot control levels of glucose (sugar) in the blood.

The best way to avoid developing Type 2 diabetes is to eat a healthy diet and take regular physical activity. This is particularly important for the increasing numbers of obese children who risk developing the condition.

However, if you already have Type 2 diabetes, you can take steps to control, and maybe reverse, the condition through diet and exercise. Improving both will also reduce the risk of complications affecting the heart, eyes, kidneys, and circulatory conditions affecting the feet.

which type?

Why weight?

A 14-year American study of nurses showed that those who gained 5–8kg (11–17lb) during that time were twice as likely to develop Type 2 diabetes. Women who gained 8–11kg (17–24lb) were three times as likely to develop the condition. By contrast, women who lost 5kg (11lb) more than halved their risk. And among women who had diabetes, those who lost 5–10 per cent of their excess weight reduced their need for medication.

Big apple

When it comes to your risk of developing Type 2 diabetes, a lot depends on where you put on weight. Are you an apple or a pear? If you carry weight around your tummy (see p25), the level of fat in your bloodstream is likely to be higher than that of people with excess weight on their hips. Raised levels of chloresterol and fats in the blood increase the risk of Type 2 diabetes. Whatever your shape, it is best to lose the excess pounds.

(see p25)

See the signs
The symptoms of diabetes are excessive thirst, frequent urination, and dehydration, as the body tries to get rid of excess glucose in the blood. In Type 2 diabetes, however, the symptoms may be less severe and so more difficult to spot. If you think that you or a member of your family may be at risk of developing diabetes, consult a doctor.

the two types of diabetes

Type 1 diabetes

The pancreas fails to produce the hormone insulin, causing blood glucose levels to rise unchecked. Type 1 affects mainly children and adolescents, but can also occur later in life. It is not linked to obesity.

Type 2 diabetes

The pancreas produces little of the hormone insulin and the body is unable to respond properly. Type 2 only used to affect older people, but is now occurring in the young. It is linked to overweight and inactivity.

Food facts

Prevent the onset of Type 2 diabetes with a healthy, balanced diet. Eat plenty of wholegrain foods high in fibre, cereals, beans, pulses, vegetables, and fruit and eat fewer high-fat and energy-dense foods to tip the balance to prevention. A healthy diet for people with Type 2 diabetes is much the same as for anyone else. Balance is the key.

How active?

Both vigorous exercise, such as running, and moderate exercise, such as walking, reduce the risk of Type 2 diabetes. Take 60–90 minutes of moderate exercise a day if you need to lose weight. If you have diabetes and use insulin, talk to your doctor or nurse about balancing food and insulin intake before and after exercise.

Our Fitness Expert says:
If you're feeling down, exercise can improve your mood and give you a great sense of wellbeing. Get up and go for it!

the **glycaemic index**

For most people with Type 2 diabetes (see pp120–121), the most important thing to concentrate on is weight loss, based on the familiar equation: calories in equals calories out. But once you have lost the weight, you could benefit from eating more foods with a low glycaemic index (GI).

The GI ranks the effect that food has on blood glucose. Carbohydrates that have a low GI are digested more slowly, releasing energy gradually, resulting in smaller rises in blood glucose and a more even energy supply – healthy whether you have Type 2 diabetes or not.

why should I go GI low?

- You'll feel fuller for longer, so that you are less hungry and less likely to overeat and put on weight
- You can help to prevent the onset of Type 2 diabetes and other conditions, such as metabolic syndrome
- You can reduce the level of fat in your blood, reducing the risk of heart disease
- If you have diabetes, you can reduce the impact of food on your blood glucose level, helping you to control your condition
- If you have diabetes, your body's sensitivity to the hormone insulin will improve, further helping you to keep your condition in check

Highs and lows

So how do you go low? Which are the low GI foods that you should be stocking up on and which are the high GI foods that you should cut down on? There are some general guidelines to follow. Most complex carbohydrates, such as pasta and wholegrains, have low GI ratings because they release their energy slowly. Most simple carbohydrates such as chocolate confectionery and sweets have a high GI because they provide a "sugar rush", releasing energy quickly and for a short time. You don't need to stop eating high (and medium) GI foods completely – this would be very difficult, if not impossible. It's all about combining foods and finding a healthy balance. See p157 for a list of some of the most common low, medium, and high GI foods.

Surprising GI ratings

Stop press! Wholemeal bread, baked potatoes, rice cakes, and plain boiled rice all have high GI ratings – yet they are healthy, nutritious foods that help control hunger. However, wholegrain, multi-grain, and rye bread have low GI scores, as do basmati rice, pasta, cold potatoes, porridge, and muesli. What's the difference? The answer is all to do with chemistry. Combinations of ingredients and chemical changes that occur during cooking all have a bearing on GI. For example, starch contained in basmati rice is chemically different to the starch in other types of rice, so it has a lower GI. And the starch in hot potatoes is digested quicker than the starch in cold potatoes, so hot potatoes have a higher GI. Foods that seem to be low may be higher than you think.

GI go!
Don't try to limit your diet to low GI foods only, because you need the nutrients from all good foods. However, it is a good idea to choose low GI for foods that are eaten on their own, such as snacks, so grab a banana (for example) if you're genuinely hungry between meals.

balance

preventing **heart disease**

There is a lot you can do to change unhealthy habits and reduce your risk of heart attack and stroke. Women as well as men need to act – perhaps surprisingly, women are more likely to die from heart and circulatory disease than men, but at a later age.

Being overweight, unhealthy diets high in saturated fat, smoking, and a sedentary lifestyle are the leading causes of coronary heart disease and stroke. These health problems can cause about 10 years of disability in later life.

Simple lifestyle changes could help prevent many people dying or being disabled each year from heart disease and stroke.

The best defence

Take regular physical activity and have a healthy BMI of between 18.5 and 25 (to calculate your BMI, see p25), and eat at least five varied portions of fruit and vegetables each day. Other heart-protective foods include oily fish and high-fibre foods such as wholegrains and pulses, which help to lower cholesterol. Pulses, such as soya, and green leafy vegetables also contain the B vitamin folate that helps protect the heart.

How active should I be?

To improve your heart function and circulation and protect against heart disease and stroke, you need to do at least 30 minutes of moderate to vigorous exercise a day. Be sure to avoid sudden bursts of high-intensity exercise, for example during sports such as squash, especially if you do not take regular exercise or if you have a heart condition.

The pressure's on

Weight control through life is the key to avoiding raised blood pressure. If you have a blood pressure with a reading consistently more than 140/90 mm Hg, your risk of stroke and heart problems increases. The naturally occurring mineral potassium, that can be gained from eating fruit and vegetables on a daily basis, actively helps to regulate blood pressure (see pp68–71 for more sources).

Smoke screen

The younger a person begins to smoke, the greater the risk of eventually contracting smoking-related heart disease. The overwhelming majority of smokers begin tobacco use before they reach the age of ten. Half of the world's children are exposed to second-hand smoke. If you smoke, stop now for you and those around you (see pp134–135 for help).

Reduce to reduce
People with high blood pressure who are obese see a fall of 1–2mmHg for every 1kg (2lb) weight they lose.

keep blood pressure in check

- Stop smoking
- Lose weight
- Take regular aerobic exercise
- Don't drink too much alcohol
- Eat 5-a-day fruits and vegetables
- Reduce your salt intake to less than 5g (1 tsp) a day

Act early
Obese children are 3 times more likely to go on to have high blood pressure, a risk for heart disease, than non-obese children. Just one kingsize chocolate bar provides a fifth of the daily calorie needs for a 10 year old – cut it out!

cholesterol – **friend or foe?**

Two out of three adults in the UK have an unhealthy level of cholesterol in their blood, yet few are aware that high cholesterol is a risk factor for heart disease and can contribute to stroke.

Eating a lot of high-fat foods contributes to a build up of cholesterol and plaque, which narrows and hardens the artery walls and is the main cause of coronary heart disease. Raised cholesterol also makes blood more likely to clot and blocks blood flow to the heart, causing heart attack or, if it happens in the brain, stroke.

But some cholesterol has a protective effect. Taking enough exercise and eating a balanced low-fat diet can lower total cholesterol and improve your ratio of good to bad cholesterol.

which foods contain cholesterol?

Try to keep your intake below 300mg a day

1 medium egg – 200 mg	1 fried chicken wing – 45mg
1 portion breaded scampi – 185mg	1 portion shelled prawns – 3mg
1 portion beef mince – 88mg	1 tbsp cream – 15mg
1 lean pork steak – 65mg	1 biscuit – 12 mg
1 portion cheddar cheese – 45mg	

Good, bad, and ugly

High-density lipoprotein (HDL) is a beneficial cholesterol that helps to protect your arteries from clogging. It is made naturally in the body. Low-density lipoprotein (LDL) and Very low-density lipoprotein (VLDL) are the harmful types of cholesterol that can clog your arteries. The higher your HDL to LDL ratio, the better. If your total cholesterol level is unhealthily high, please see your doctor for advice. You may be recommended a low-fat or low-cholesterol diet, and encouraged to exercise more. Or you may require medication.

What shouldn't I eat?

Foods that contain cholesterol, such as eggs, cheese, cream, seafood, and meat do raise blood cholesterol levels, but the rise is generally small. A more effective way of lowering blood cholesterol is to reduce the total amount of fat in your diet, especially saturated and trans fats found in biscuits, cakes, full-fat dairy products, and hydrogenated (hardened) vegetable fats.

What should I eat?

Oats, beans, soya products, wholegrains, and some fruit and vegetables contain soluble fibre, which can help to lower LDL cholesterol. Some spreads and foods such as yoghurts and drinks that contain plant stanols and sterols can help to lower cholesterol when eaten as part of a low-fat diet. Folate also has a protective effect. Food sources of folate include green leafy vegetables (broccoli, Brussels sprouts, spinach, and spring greens), wholegrains, pulses (black eye and baked beans), and breakfast cereals fortified with folic acid and vitamins B6 and B12.

The benefits of exercise

Being much more physically active can make a huge difference to your cholesterol levels. Vigorous exercise is more effective at lowering harmful LDL cholesterol than moderate levels. Do three 20-minute bouts of vigorous exercise a week to have the most beneficial effect. This could be anything from jogging, to skipping, to dancing the salsa – you choose.

choice

Know your number
A simple pin-prick blood test can reveal your blood cholesterol level. The average blood cholesterol for a British adult is 6.2 millimoles per litre (mml/l). In the UK a healthy cholesterol level is considered to be 5.2 mml/l or below (the World Health Organisation figure is 3.8). Ask your doctor for individual advice.

Home in on homocysteine
Just as a high level of cholesterol can cause heart risk, so can homocysteine. Homocysteine is an amino acid – a by-product of protein breakdown, found in proteins and some pulses. It is being dubbed "the new cholesterol", as it has been found to damage arteries and contribute to cholesterol build up. It can be rendered harmless, however, by folates and other B vitamins, so eat more of the foods containing them (see left for the best sources).

fats for a **healthy heart**

Eating less high-fat food is an important step not only towards losing weight, but also towards reducing the risk of heart disease. But not all fats are bad, and some essential fats even help to protect the heart, partly by helping to reduce the level of harmful cholesterol in the blood (see pp126–127). The trick is to identify the good and the bad fats and to strike the right balance between them.

Put simply, unsaturated fats make the blood less sticky and less likely to cause a heart attack or stroke. The two types of beneficial unsaturated fats are polyunsaturated and monounsaturated. Saturated fats and trans fats are the harmful fats that cause problems for the heart.

protection

The fats of the matter

Good fats

- Polyunsaturated fats include essential fatty acids, of which there are two types. Omega-6 linoleic acid is found in sunflower, soya, corn, and safflower oils and helps to reduce blood cholesterol. Omega-3 linolenic acid is found in oily fish, rapeseed oil, walnuts, and some green leafy vegetables. It "thins" the blood, making it less likely to clot and cause a heart attack or stroke.

- Monounsaturated fats are good because they, too, can help to lower the level of harmful cholesterol and increase the level of beneficial cholesterol in the blood. They are not as effective as polyunsaturated fats, however. The best known source of monounsaturated is olive oil, but it is also found in rapeseed oil, nuts (especially walnuts), and avocados.

Bad fats

- Saturated fats are usually found in animal foods such as meat, cream, cheese, and milk. Hardened fats such as block margarine and other cooking fats, including lard and butter, are mainly saturated fats and they are found in foods such as pastries, biscuits, deep-fried foods, crisps, chips, meat pies, and some meat products, such as sausages.

- Trans fats start out as unsaturated, but are hydrogenated (hardened) for food processing and cooking and to increase shelf life. They raise your cholesterol level even more than saturated fats. Look out for trans fats on ingredients labels – they are sometimes listed as hydrogenated fat. These fats are often found in spreads, cooking fats, biscuits, cakes, pies, pastries, savoury snacks, and readymeals.

Miss Chiplash says: Sardines are cheap and easy oily fish. Buy them tinned (in water or tomato sauce, and have them on toast followed by a yoghurt for a light meal or snack.

helping to prevent **cancer**

The increase in the incidence of some cancers in the UK has been blamed on obesity. Diet, including being overweight, accounts for about 30 per cent of cancers, making it second only to smoking as a preventable cause of cancer.

Obese people are 25–30 per cent more likely to develop colon cancer, prostate cancer, endometrial cancer, oesophageal cancer, kidney cancer, and post-menopausal breast cancer. Cancer of the endometrium (lining of the womb) is three times higher among obese women than slim women. Being overweight also increases the risk of breast cancer among post-menopausal women. With this information, you can reduce the risk of developing certain cancers by eating the right foods and becoming more physically active.

beat it

Half the risk
A 12-year trial in which overweight American women lost at least 9kg (20lb) showed that they halved their chance of dying from obesity-related cancers.

Obesity and sex hormones

When you have a lot of body fat, your body produces more sex hormones. Sex hormones influence cell division in areas such as the breast and endometrium in women and the prostate in men. The higher the level of sex hormones, the more potential there is for problems, because the more frequently cells divide, the greater the chance of cancer occurring.

Eat the right foods

Eating vegetables and fruit is important. Regularly choose orange fruit and vegetables such as carrots, apricots, melon, and squash, red and purple berries, and dark green leafy vegetables. Also, include wholegrains, pulses, and soya foods in your diet. Eat more fish – particularly oily fish such as sardines and pilchards. Foods to avoid include high-salt foods and any food that has become charred.

Obesity and insulin

The more body fat you have, the more of the hormone insulin your body produces, and the more likely it is that you will develop insulin resistance. This means that even more insulin is produced to try to compensate for the resistance. Insulin carries sugar to the body cells, which encourages cell division, thereby further increasing the risk of cancer.

The active issue

Physical activity has a cancer-preventive effect because it reduces levels of sex hormones and insulin. As obesity is a major risk factor in cancer, as much as 60–90 minutes of exercise a day may be needed for weight control. One hour of moderate activity a day, such as a brisk walk, specifically lowers the risk for cancers of the colon and rectum. Even 30 minutes, five times a week, has prevention benefits.

Home help
Women who do more than 4 hours of housework per day have a 30 per cent lower risk of developing endometrial cancer. Another great reason for getting out your duster, plugging in the vacuum cleaner, and giving your home a clean!

what's your best defence?

- Lose weight if you need to
- Avoid gaining more than 5kg (11lb) during adult life
- Keep your waist measurement below 81cm (32in) for women and 94cm (37in) for men

- Eat at least 5 portions of a wide and colourful variety of fruit and vegetables each day
- Include wholegrains, pulses, and soya foods in your diet
- Take more exercise every day

Our Fitness Expert says:
Get physical – it really can help to protect you from developing cancer. Research shows that 4 out of 5 women are putting themselves at risk of cancer by not taking enough exercise.

the **joint effect**

By being overweight, you are making matters worse if you are at risk of, or suffer from, any condition affecting the bones or joints. Osteoporosis is demineralization and weakening of the bones – it affects one in three women in the UK, usually after the menopause. Osteoarthritis affects mainly older people, causing swelling, pain, and stiffness in the joints, and can make movement difficult if left untreated.

Being the right weight and keeping your BMI (see p25) in check will make life much easier for you if you have problems with joint and bone health. Exercising more is also beneficial for bone health, as having more muscle and less fat on your body makes it easier to build up bone density, helping to prevent or treat osteoporosis.

Calcium requirements
The Department of Health recommends a daily calcium intake of 700mg for adult women, but the National Osteoporosis Society recommends 1000mg for women aged 20-45 years, 1200mg for pregnant and breastfeeding women, and 1500mg for women over 45 – but only 1000mg if you are on HRT.

in the frame

Move to prevent

Exercise is helpful in the prevention of both osteoporosis and arthritis. While you are young, it's important to include some vigorous activity in your active life, such as running, rope skipping, or aerobics. As your bone mass deteriorates after the age of 25, you need to do weight-bearing exercise to increase your muscle strength and bone health. Using weights helps bones because it places an impact on them, helping to build them up.

Activity and arthritis

It's a myth that physical activity can wear out arthritic joints. However, it can be painful if you overdo it and during acute attacks you need to take it very easy. Don't be put off, however – it's important that you ride it out and continue to exercise to improve your mobility, flexibility, and muscle strength, as well as keeping up fitness.

Move to improve

If you already have a bone or joint condition, exercise helps to prevent stiffness, increases movement, strengthens muscles, and can boost your mood. Take moderate physical activity regularly. The best thing that you can do is walk briskly for 30 minutes every day.

You are my sunshine

There are many foods that are recommended for bone health (see below). Foods such as dairy products, margarine, and fish oils are particularly good as they contain vitamin D – excellent for strong bones. Take as much exercise as you can in the fresh air too, because sunlight on the skin makes vitamin D in the body. In the summer, 15–20 minutes a day of being in the sun (not sunbathing) is sufficient to produce enough vitamin D for a whole year.

Cod liver oil
Some people who suffer from osteoarthritis find that cod liver oil supplements can improve joint movement, alleviate the pain, and reduce the damage to joints, because the omega-3 fatty acids in fish oil are anti-inflammatory.

eat more...

- Plant proteins such as beans, nuts, seeds, and wholegrains
- Oily fish, such as sardines, mackerel, and pilchards
- Fruit and vegetables, which create a more alkaline (less acidic) body chemistry, strengthening bones

avoid...

- Fizzy drinks, coffee, and cola, which can cause calcium loss if you are at risk
- Salt and alcohol, which reduce the body's ability to absorb and retain calcium

Miss Chiplash says:
We need calcium for healthy bones. In addition to milk, yoghurt, and cheese, less well-known sources of calcium are bread (there's more in white bread than brown bread because white flour is fortified with calcium), green leafy vegetables, and beans – even baked beans.

no **smoking**

Healthy living messages always involve not smoking, and for good reason. Smoking has a huge impact on increasing your risk of long-term disease. For example, it quadruples the risk of stroke and, when combined with high blood pressure, the risk increases eightfold. Smoking is also the most common cause of cancer and makes osteoporosis worse – the list is endless...

Yet amazingly, in the face of logic, the fallacy persists that smoking is a good way to control appetite and, therefore, prevent weight gain.

While weight control is important in preventing heart disease, Type 2 diabetes, and other conditions, it can never justify smoking as a slimming aid because it has far too many other health risks. Smoking does not ultimately help weight loss. While it might suppress appetite and speed up your metabolic rate (the rate at which calories are used), the effect is short-lived – and so are you!

pack it in

Our Psychologist says:
Tell yourself that you are finished with being a smoker and want to live longer and healthier. Set a quit date. Throw out all smoking-related stuff and deal with urges to smoke by going for a walk, or doing some other form of exercise, and taking some long, deep breaths. If you are really struggling, see your doctor for advice on supports and medication.

I'll get fat if I quit!

Weight gain is not inevitable when you stop smoking – especially if you know what to expect and are prepared. Smoking increases your metabolic rate, so when you give up, you will need fewer calories – in other words, less food – to maintain the same weight. It is fine to carry on eating the same amount as before, but stick to portion control (see pp32–35) and stock up on slimming snacks – plenty of fruit, low-fat yoghurts or other desserts, high-fibre biscuits and crispbreads, low-fat scones, or tea breads. Also, drink lots of water and other drinks (non-alcoholic).

How can exercise help?

Increasing the amount of physical activity you do will help to reduce any stress associated with giving up, improve your mood, and take your mind off smoking. Choose activity-based evening events such as ten-pin bowling or rollerskating rather than going to the pub or the restaurant, where the temptation to light up may be too great. By being more active, you will also work off any extra weight that you may have gained as a result of quitting. You'll quickly notice how much easier exercise becomes once you've given up smoking, as your lung capacity and heart health increase.

things can only get better...

- After 20 minutes, your blood pressure and pulse rate begin to return to normal and the circulation in your hands and feet will improve
- After 24 hours, the nicotine will have left your body and your lungs will begin to clear out mucus and debris
- After 1 week, you will notice that there is more money in your wallet or purse and your hair and clothes won't smell of smoke

- After 3–9 months, coughing and shortness of breath will subside and your overall lung function will have improved by 5–10 per cent
- After 5 years, your risk of heart attack will have fallen to about half that of a smoker
- After 10 years, your risk of lung cancer will have fallen to around half that of a smoker and your risk of heart attack will have fallen to about the same as someone who has never smoked

the alcohol **question**

Common sense tells us there is a connection between weight gain and alcohol – you are no doubt familiar with what is lovingly referred to as the "beer belly". Yet brewers argue that it is bar snacks and post-pub curries, and not the beer, that pile on the pounds.

In general, the more you drink, the more you weigh, or the higher your BMI (see p25). The fact is that alcohol contains 7 calories per gram, which is much more than carbohydrates and protein and only slightly less than fat, which contains 9 calories per gram. Remember – calories in should equal calories out (and that includes alcohol).

moderation

don't drink more than...

Women	Men
21 units a week	28 units a week
2–3 drinks a day	3–4 drinks a day

Isn't alcohol good for me?

The health benefits of alcohol are rather exaggerated. While people who drink one unit a day may be likely to live longer than non-drinkers and moderate-to-heavy drinkers, few people really benefit. The heart and stroke protection benefits have only been proved in post-menopausal women – sorry to disappoint everyone else.

What's in it?

Alcohol is not regarded as a nutrient. Its intoxicating and addictive effect make it too dangerous to recommend. But traditional beers and stouts are a good source of B vitamins, and red wines, particularly those made in sunnier climates, are a good source of antioxidants, which may help to protect against heart disease and some cancers.

What's the reality?

Drinking alcohol contributes to overweight and obesity, particularly in men. While alcoholics are usually thinner than average, non-dependent drinkers are usually overweight, and the fact that they carry weight around their waists (in the form of beer bellies) puts them at greater risk of Type 2 diabetes and heart disease. Alcohol intake has increased dramatically in young women, resulting in increased cases of cirrhosis of the liver.

Measure for measure

Bars and pubs may be encouraging you to drink more. Many advertise "three for the price of two" when you buy a large glass of wine or drink it at "happy hour". Staff may also encourage you to choose larger glasses of wine and pitchers of beer. And measures are creeping up, too. Good value? Not for your waistline or your health.

Wine not?

A glass of wine is now more likely to be 175ml than the standard 125ml that contains one unit of alcohol. The standard size 125ml glass of red wine contains 116 calories, while the larger 175ml glass is 162 calories and the 250ml glass, nearly 250 calories!

Spirited away

The serving size of spirits in pubs is now often 35ml (as opposed to the standard measure of 25ml). There is now 20 extra calories per shot of vodka, whisky, and other spirits.

Our Psychologist says:
Make sure you keep an eye on how many units of alcohol you drink each week and set a maximum target. Space your drinking with non-alcoholic "spacers" and avoid salty snacks, which make you thirsty and encourage you to drink more. Aim for at least two alcohol-free days a week and avoid bingeing at the weekend. Keep an alcohol diary if you're not sure how much you're drinking (see p154).

rounders challenge

It's the game you haven't played since school – it's the game that anyone can play. Instead of going to the pub at lunchtime or after work, round up your friends and family for a game of rounders at the local park or sports centre. Batting and fielding, you'll soon work off that beer belly!

what's on your list?

You now have the information you need to **balance your diet** and be **more active** to control your weight and avoid the health risks associated with overweight. The choice is now yours. With all the **positive benefits** awaiting you, it's a "no brainer". So, get planning, get organizing, and get going…

TO DO:
* WALK DOG
* BUY FISH FOR DINNER
* MOW LAWN
* GYM TONIGHT

your **personal eating plan**

Whether you want to lose weight or maintain your healthy weight, you can work out your calorie needs to tailor-make a personal eating plan for your needs.

what your plan includes

1 a **resting metabolic rate** (RMR) – the calories you use when you are resting

2 the **number of calories** you need to eat every day in order to lose weight or maintain your healthy weight

3 **calorie counting** made easy with portion guides for everyday eating

4 variations on the portion theme, to give you **greater flexibility** in your eating

5 how to **plan your portions** at meal times so that you can sensibly fit your portions into your day

3 steps to your plan

To work out how many calories you need per day to maintain your weight and not put on (or regain) any extra pounds, or if you need to lose weight, follow the three simple steps below. This will give you your own personal daily calorie needs. Stick to these to keep your weight under control. If you want to speed up your weight loss, or eat a little more and not put on weight, make sure you do your daily 30 minutes to 1 hour of moderate exercise (see pp144–149). The most important thing is to enjoy your healthy eating regime – it will soon become second nature and you won't even have to think about it – and look forward to opening the door to a slimmer, brighter, and healthier you.

Stick to the plan
Don't be tempted to cut more calories or portions than is advised in this plan in an effort to lose more weight quickly. Your personal eating plan has been carefully worked out for effective and long-term weight loss and by cutting corners, you'll be cutting the benefits, too.

1. Work out your personal resting metabolic rate (RMR) by doing the following calculation

Age	Men	Women
18–30 years	15.3 x weight (kg) +679	14.7 x weight (kg) +496
30–60 years	11.6 x weight (kg) +879	8.7 x weight (kg) +829
60 years +	13.5 x weight (kg) +487	10.5 x weight (kg) +596

2. Work out your activity level

   Inactive (mainly sedentary all day and evening) = **1.3**

   Lightly active (some activity, walking, housework, general chores) = **1.4**

   Moderately active (most of the time on your feet, or regular moderate exercise 3 or 4 times a week) = **1.5**

3. Do the sum

   RMR x activity level = 0000 calories

   This is the number of calories you need to eat daily in order to keep your weight stable. If you need to lose weight, subtract 500–600 calories from the answer. This gives you the number of calories you need to eat on a daily basis to lose weight.

calorie counted meals made easy

Instead of taking away your daily calorie needs and having to work out how many calories you are eating each day, use the easy portion guide below. If your calorie needs for weight loss are more than 2400 calories a day, ask your family doctor to refer you to a state-registered dietitian.

calories and food group portions

Daily cals	1200	1300	1400	1500	1600	1700	1800	1900	2000	2100	2200	2300	2400
*Starch	5	5	5	6	6	6	7	7	8	8	9	9	9
Fruit	2	2	3	3	3	3	3	3	3	3	3	4	4
Vegetables	4	4	4	4	4	4	4	4	4	4	5	5	5
*Protein	4	5	5	6	6	7	7	8	8	8	8	9	9
Milk	2	2	2	2	2	2.5	2.5	2.5	3	3	3	3	3
Fat	3	3	3	3	4	4	4	4	4	5	5	5	6
Snacks (cals)	50	100	100	100	150	150	150	150	150	200	200	200	250

*Swap to make 4 starch and 5 protein if you prefer.

protein portions

You may think that there are more protein portions on the eating plan than you would expect. The reason is that the protein portion sizes in this plan are smaller than those for a normal main meal, to allow for more flexibility. For other food group portions, use the portion sizes on pp34–35.

Meat, fish, and protein alternatives

These are cooked weights for meat, fish, and beans. Uncooked weights will be around 25 per cent heavier.

Lean beef, pork, lamb, chicken, or turkey	28g or 1 thin slice
Ham (no fat)	42g 1½oz
Chicken casserole	56g (2oz)
Bolognese sauce or chilli	56g (2oz)
White fish, seafood, or vegetable-based meat alternative	56g (2oz)
Oily fish (mackerel, salmon)	28g (1oz)
Fish finger	1
Bacon	1 lean rasher
Egg	1
Beans. lentils, baked beans, tofu	2 tbsp
Nuts, seeds, or nut butter	1 tsp
Houmus (reduced-fat)	1 rounded tbsp
Hard cheese, edam, or brie	28g (1oz)

meal planner

Fill in your personal meal planner from the calorie guide, left.

No. of portions	Food group
	Starch (bread, potatoes, pasta, rice, and cereals)
	Fruit
	Vegetables
	Protein (meat, fish, and protein alternatives)
	Milk (and cheese and yoghurt)
	Fat (including oils, dressings, and spreads)
	Snacks (see calories guide)

daily portion plan

You might find it helpful to see how your allocated number of portions can fit into a day's eating. This is for 1700 calories a day. Don't worry – you might not always match the target in each category – the example below shows an extra piece of fruit as a snack.

Time	Food/drink	Starch	Protein	Fruit	Veg	Milk	Fat	Snacks
07.30	Orange juice			1				
	Porridge	1						
	1 slice toast and spread	1					1	
11.00	Cereal bar	1						
	Latte					2		
13.00	Avocado and		1		2			
	bacon salad vinaigrette							
	slice bread and spread	1					2	
15.00	1 orange			1				150 cals
16.00	Tea (without milk)							
	1 biscuit	1						100 cals
20.00	Chicken leg, rice,	1	5					
	carrots, and peas				2			
	Fruit salad with yoghurt			2		0.5-1		
Total for day		**6**	**6**	**4**	**4**	**2.5**	**0–3**	**250 cals**
Target		**6**	**7**	**3**	**4**	**2.5**	**0–3**	**150 cals**

Stay hydrated
Remember, you need to drink at least 6–8 glasses of liquid per day. Most of this should be water but, for the sake of variety, you can supplement it with diet soft drinks, fruit and herbal teas, tea, or coffee (with milk from the number of portions allocated to your personal eating plan).

what's on your list? 143

your **fitness programme**

If you need to lose weight, choose fat-burning exercises to do in conjunction with eating a balanced diet. The best exercise for fat-burning is jogging, followed by cycling, walking, aerobics and other specialized exercise classes, such as step or circuit training.

top **fat-busting** activities

1 even a **brisk walk** can have fat-busting benefits – you can build up from there

2 **hop on your bike,** buckle your helmet, and go for a speedy spin

3 get your trainers on and **jog or run** off the fat at the park or in the gym

4 an **aerobics class** is a fun, sociable way of shedding the pounds

5 step up to a trimmer you with an energetic **step class** – up, up, and away!

The science bit

Fat can only be burned in the presence of oxygen – during aerobic exercise. When the demands of exercise increase beyond the speed at which the body can burn fat using oxygen, it switches to the anaerobic system, which stops burning body fat and burns glycogen (energy stored in the liver) instead. Make it aerobic exercise, in which you breathe quicker, to burn the fat.

Work less hard to lose fat

Whichever activity you choose, you need to do it at a moderate intensity for fat to be burned as fuel. If you work at a higher level you gain the health benefits of improved heart fitness and circulation benefits, but you do not necessarily burn fat. As a general rule, to burn fat, work at 50 per cent or 70 per cent of your maximum heart rate. To do your fat-burning maths see below.

fat-burning maths

Sedentary unfit people need to work at around 50 per cent of their maximum heart rate and fit people at up to 70 per cent. To predict your maximum heart rate, follow these steps (this example is for an unfit **40** year old – so he or she needs to work at **50 per cent** of his or her maximum heart rate):

1. 220 minus **40** (age) = 180 (maximum heart rate)

2. 180 minus 85 (resting heart rate) = 95

3. To calculate **50 per cent** of 95: 95 x 0.50 = 47.5 + 85 (resting heart rate) = 132 target heart rate for fat burning

Feel the beat

You need to take your pulse during and immediately after exercising to check whether you are working at the optimum fat-burning level. Use either your wrist or the side of your neck. Count for ten seconds as you feel the beat and multiply the number of beats by six to find your beats per minute.

- **Wrist** Place the tips of your index and middle fingers on the inside of your wrist in line with your thumb and press lightly
- **Neck** Place the tips of your index and middle fingers on the side of your neck just below your jaw and to the left or right of your windpipe and press lightly

The programmes

Your present level of health and fitness should determine where you start on these fitness programmes. But don't feel downhearted if you are less fit or carry too much weight, because you are likely to improve at the greatest rate and see the fastest results. Exercise for a minimum of 30 minutes and a maximum of 1 hour. If you are a beginner, limit the core part of your programme to 15 minutes to start with and include recovery time of 1–2 minutes if you need to. To guarantee successful weight loss, do your programme 2–4 times a week – in addition to being active in your daily life and eating less.

getting the most from the programmes

- Start at the right level for your current weight and fitness

- Make sure you warm up before the activity and warm down afterwards

- Start slowly and build up your level of fitness steadily

- Exercise for 30 minutes at the least and 1 hour at the most

- Ask a friend or a family member to accompany you on your walk or run – you may need the encouragement

- Make sure you do your routine 2–4 times a week – no excuses!

- Enjoy it! Being out and about and getting your heart and lungs working is fun – and you'll reap the rewards as a trimmer you

Warm up to warm down

Warm up All exercise should start with a gentle warm up, during which you do your chosen activity at a slower rate to get your circulation going and your muscles working. The warm up needs to last for about 10–20 per cent of the exercise time. **Core time** This follows the warm up and is when you work at the maximum level you have chosen. For fat burning, this needs to be at 50–70 per cent of your maximum heart rate (see pp144–145).
Warm down is as important as the warm up. Instead of stopping suddenly, which might make you feel faint, gradually decrease the intensity of the exercise, and then stretch out your muscles to prevent any soreness.

Fat-burning routines

LEVEL ONE – WALKING

If you are not used to exercise and are starting out, begin here. Do the programme 5 times a week and then you can build it up.

	Warm up	Core time	Warm down
Beginners	walk slowly	walk briskly	walk slowly
Week 1	5 minutes	5 minutes	5 minutes
Week 2	5 minutes	8 minutes	5 minutes
Week 3	5 minutes	15 minutes	5 minutes
Week 4	5 minutes	20 minutes	5 minutes

	Warm up	Core time	Warm down
Intermediate	steady pace	walk briskly	walk slowly
Week 1	5 minutes	15 minutes	5 minutes
Week 2	5 minutes	20 minutes	5 minutes
Week 3	5 minutes	25 minutes	5 minutes
Week 4	5 minutes	30 minutes	5 minutes

LEVEL TWO – JOGGING

You are ready to go up a level, so get going and do this programme 4 times a week, resting on alternate days. Don't forget to stretch afterwards.

	Warm up	Core time	Warm down
Beginners	walk slowly	walk briskly	walk slowly
Week 1	5 minutes	walk 9 mins, jog 1 min	5 minutes
Week 2	5 minutes	walk 5 mins jog 3, repeat	5 minutes
Week 3	5 minutes	walk 4 mins, jog 5, repeat	5 minutes
Week 4	5 minutes	walk 3 mins, jog 8, repeat	5 minutes

Mix it up
After the first month of walking, try some strength or resistance training and flexibility exercises in addition to your programme. Walking is great exercise and an excellent place to start, but it does not help joint flexibility – you need to supplement your programme with dance, step, or martial arts classes, for example, to really get you pumping!

Time out
When you have a cold or
any other minor infection
it is wise to reduce the
amount of activity you do
and rest. There's no point
in pushing on through
illness, as your body will not
benefit and you may end up
aggravating your condition.
Rest up and you'll soon be
back up to speed.

LEVEL TWO – JOGGING Intermediate

Give this level a try when you can manage 20 minutes of non-stop jogging.
Stretch after exercising to prevent muscle soreness.

	Warm up	Core time	Warm down
	walk slowly	jog	slow to walk
Monday	5 minutes	20 minutes	5 minutes
Tuesday	Rest day (but do another activity)		
Wednesday	5 minutes	jog fast 5 mins slow 1–2, repeat twice	5 minutes
Thursday	Rest day (but do another activity)		
Friday	5 minutes	25 minutes steady pace	5 minutes
Saturday	Rest day (but do another activity)		
Sunday	5 minutes	25 minutes steady pace	

LEVEL THREE – RUNNING

If you have mastered walking and jogging, you're ready to progress to
running. Monitor your heart rate (HR) and stretch afterwards!

	Warm up	Core time	Warm down
	jog slowly	jog quickly	slow to walk
Monday	5 minutes	25 mins 70% HR	5 minutes
Tuesday	Rest day (but do another activity)		
Wednesday	5 minutes	35 mins 75–80% HR	5 minutes
Thursday	Rest day (but do another activity)		
Friday	5 minutes	60 mins 75% HR	5 minutes
Saturday	Rest day (but do another activity)		
Sunday	5 minutes	2 mins 75% HR 2 mins 60%, repeat 5 times	5 minutes

Our Fitness Expert says:
If your favourite activities
are yoga, Pilates or classes
for "abs" or "bums and
tums", watch out! While
these have their benefits,
they are not fat-burning
(apart from very energetic
ashtanga yoga). If
you enjoy them
carry on, but
supplement
them with
a fat-burning
programme or
classes.

have an active week

If you want a fun week of activity, take things up a step and work on all aspects of your fitness.

- **Metabolic Monday** Have a brisk walk or jog twice a day to keep your metabolic rate high
- **Triathlon Tuesday** Do three different and varied activities, such as a cycle ride, brisk walk or jog, and a swim – you choose the distance and intensity
- **Workout Wednesday** Follow your usual walking, jogging, or running programme
- **Tone-up Thursday** Do some light weight work for 20 minutes – at the gym or at home
- **Freedom Friday** Take a day off and T.G.I.F
- **Step it up Saturday** Do your hardest regular workout of the previous week
- **Sit back Sunday** Another day of well-earned rest (or make it Swim Sunday if you really want some action)

Programme plus

While you are following your fitness programme, you need to supplement your routine with other activities to make up your daily exercise needs. There is a host of activities to choose from that can help to burn fat as well as improving your flexibility and strength. Aerobics classes help to burn fat, whether high-impact (in which both feet leave the ground) or low-impact (feet don't leave the ground). Dance classes have to be a combination of workout and dance movements to burn fat and be aerobic. Jazz-based, salsa, or similar lively dance classes will burn fat. They also improve coordination and increase flexibility.

Step classes burn fat and can be done at varying aerobic intensity. The choreographed workout needs good coordination and there are muscle-building benefits. Boxercise and Kick classes combine martial arts with aerobics, step, and boxing – great all-rounders.

bottoms-up challenge

OK, so it's a rainy day, there's no babysitter, and you just can't get out to do your fitness programme or go to the gym. That's no excuse – there is always an opportunity for buttock clenching. Sitting or standing – get up and get squeezing – wherever you are. The more you squeeze, the more toned and shapely your bum will become!

The **charts**

The following pages will give you all the extra information you need to identify your goals, organize yourself, and plan your weight loss. There are also charts for monitoring your progress, so you can congratulate yourself on your continuing success!

why **planning** matters

1 you need to **assess** your personal circumstances accurately before you begin

2 it's important to **identify your weight loss goal**, so that you know what you are aiming for

3 you can arm yourself with the knowledge you need to **plan your portions** (and your shopping!)

4 the more **choices** you have, the more varied and interesting your meal times will be

5 by charting your progress, you will **stay in control** and be inspired to succeed

BMI for adults

Measuring your body mass index (BMI)

1. Measure your height and weight in metric or imperial (whichever is easier).
2. Trace a straight horizontal line from your weight and a vertical line from your height.
3. The point at which the two lines cross indicates your BMI.
4. Decide if you need to gain weight, lose weight, or maintain your healthy weight.

Less than 18.5 = Underweight
18.5–24.9 = Ideal or healthy weight
25–29.9 = Overweight
30–39.9 = Obese
40+ = Extremely (morbidly) obese

Weight				Height																			
British	US	SI	ft ins		4' 6"	4' 8"	4' 10"	5' 0"	5' 2"	5' 3"	5' 4"	5' 5"	5' 6"	5' 7"	5' 8"	5' 9"	5' 10"	5' 11"	6' 0"	6' 2"	6' 4"	6' 6"	6' 8"
Stones	lbs	pounds	Kilos	cm	137	142	147	152	157	160	163	165	168	170	173	175	178	180	183	188	193	198	203
6	7	91	41		22.0	20.4	19.0	17.8	16.6	16.1	15.6	15.1	14.7	14.3	13.8	13.4	13.1	12.7	12.3	11.7	11.1	10.5	10.0
6	10	94	43		22.7	21.1	19.6	18.4	17.2	16.7	16.1	15.6	15.2	14.7	14.3	13.9	13.5	13.1	12.7	12.1	11.4	10.9	10.3
7	0	98	44		23.7	22.0	20.5	19.1	17.9	17.4	16.8	16.3	15.8	15.3	14.9	14.5	14.1	13.7	13.3	12.6	11.9	11.3	10.8
7	3	101	46		24.4	22.6	21.1	19.7	18.5	17.9	17.3	16.8	16.3	15.8	15.4	14.9	14.5	14.1	13.7	13.0	12.3	11.7	11.1
7	7	105	48		25.4	23.5	21.9	20.5	19.2	18.6	18.0	17.5	16.9	16.4	16.0	15.5	15.1	14.6	14.2	13.5	12.8	12.1	11.5
7	10	108	49		26.1	24.2	22.6	21.1	19.8	19.1	18.5	18.0	17.4	16.9	16.4	15.9	15.5	15.1	14.6	13.9	13.1	12.5	11.9
8	0	112	51		27.1	25.1	23.4	21.9	20.5	19.8	19.2	18.6	18.1	17.5	17.0	16.5	16.1	15.6	15.2	14.4	13.6	12.9	12.3
8	3	115	52		27.8	25.8	24.0	22.5	21.0	20.4	19.7	19.1	18.6	18.0	17.5	17.0	16.5	16.0	15.6	14.8	14.0	13.3	12.6
8	7	119	54		28.8	26.7	24.9	23.2	21.8	21.1	20.4	19.8	19.2	18.6	18.1	17.6	17.1	16.6	16.1	15.3	14.5	13.8	13.1
8	10	122	55		29.5	27.4	25.5	23.8	22.3	21.6	20.9	20.3	19.7	19.1	18.5	18.0	17.5	17.0	16.5	15.7	14.9	14.1	13.4
9	3	129	59		31.2	28.9	27.0	25.2	23.6	22.9	22.1	21.5	20.8	20.2	19.6	19.0	18.5	18.0	17.5	16.6	15.7	14.9	14.2
9	7	133	60		32.1	29.8	27.8	26.0	24.3	23.6	22.8	22.1	21.5	20.8	20.2	19.6	19.1	18.5	18.0	17.1	16.2	15.4	14.6
9	10	136	62		32.9	30.5	28.4	26.6	24.9	24.1	23.3	22.6	22.0	21.3	20.7	20.1	19.5	19.0	18.4	17.5	16.6	15.7	14.9
10	0	140	64		33.8	31.4	29.3	27.3	25.6	24.8	24.0	23.3	22.6	21.9	21.3	20.7	20.1	19.5	19.0	18.0	17.0	16.2	15.4
10	3	143	65		34.6	32.1	29.9	27.9	26.2	25.3	24.5	23.8	23.1	22.4	21.7	21.1	20.5	19.9	19.4	18.4	17.4	16.5	15.7
10	7	147	67		35.5	33.0	30.7	28.7	26.9	26.0	25.2	24.5	23.7	23.0	22.4	21.7	21.1	20.5	19.9	18.9	17.9	17.0	16.1
10	10	150	68		36.3	33.6	31.3	29.3	27.4	26.6	25.7	25.0	24.2	23.5	22.8	22.2	21.5	20.9	20.3	19.3	18.3	17.3	16.5
11	0	154	70		37.2	34.5	32.2	30.1	28.2	27.3	26.4	25.6	24.9	24.1	23.4	22.7	22.1	21.5	20.9	19.8	18.7	17.8	16.9
11	3	157	71		37.9	35.2	32.8	30.7	28.7	27.8	26.9	26.1	25.3	24.6	23.9	23.2	22.5	21.9	21.3	20.2	19.1	18.1	17.2
11	7	161	73		38.9	36.1	33.6	31.4	29.4	28.5	27.6	26.8	26.0	25.2	24.5	23.8	23.1	22.5	21.8	20.7	19.6	18.6	17.7
11	10	164	74		39.6	36.8	34.3	32.0	30.0	29.1	28.2	27.3	26.5	25.7	24.9	24.2	23.5	22.9	22.2	21.1	20.0	19.0	18.0
12	0	168	76		40.6	37.7	35.1	32.8	30.7	29.8	28.8	28.0	27.1	26.3	25.5	24.8	24.1	23.4	22.8	21.6	20.4	19.4	18.5
12	3	171	78		41.3	38.3	35.7	33.4	31.3	30.3	29.4	28.5	27.6	26.8	26.0	25.3	24.5	23.8	23.2	22.0	20.8	19.8	18.8
12	7	175	79		42.3	39.2	36.6	34.2	32.0	31.0	30.0	29.1	28.2	27.4	26.6	25.8	25.1	24.4	23.7	22.5	21.3	20.2	19.2
12	10	178	81		43.0	39.9	37.2	34.8	32.6	31.5	30.6	29.6	28.7	27.9	27.1	26.3	25.5	24.8	24.1	22.9	21.7	20.6	19.6
13	0	182	83		44.0	40.8	38.0	35.5	33.3	32.2	31.2	30.3	29.4	28.5	27.7	26.9	26.1	25.4	24.7	23.4	22.2	21.0	20.0
13	3	185	84		44.7	41.5	38.7	36.1	33.8	32.8	31.8	30.8	29.9	29.0	28.1	27.3	26.5	25.8	25.1	23.8	22.5	21.4	20.3
13	7	189	86		45.7	42.4	39.5	36.9	34.6	33.5	32.4	31.5	30.5	29.6	28.7	27.9	27.1	26.4	25.6	24.3	23.0	21.8	20.8
13	10	192	87		46.4	43.0	40.1	37.5	35.1	34.0	33.0	31.9	31.0	30.1	29.2	28.4	27.5	26.8	26.0	24.7	23.4	22.2	21.1
14	0	196	89		47.4	43.9	41.0	38.3	35.8	34.7	33.6	32.6	31.6	30.7	29.8	28.9	28.1	27.3	26.6	25.2	23.9	22.6	21.5
14	3	199	90		48.1	44.6	41.6	38.9	36.4	35.3	34.2	33.1	32.1	31.2	30.3	29.4	28.6	27.8	27.0	25.5	24.2	23.0	21.9
14	7	203	92		49.1	45.5	42.4	39.6	37.1	36.0	34.8	33.8	32.8	31.8	30.9	30.0	29.1	28.3	27.5	26.1	24.7	23.5	22.3
14	10	206	93		49.8	46.2	43.1	40.2	37.7	36.5	35.4	34.3	33.2	32.3	31.3	30.4	29.6	28.7	27.9	26.4	25.1	23.8	22.6
15	0	210	95		50.8	47.1	43.9	41.0	38.4	37.2	36.0	34.9	33.9	32.9	31.9	31.0	30.1	29.3	28.5	27.0	25.6	24.3	23.1
15	3	213	97		51.5	47.8	44.5	41.6	39.0	37.7	36.6	35.4	34.4	33.4	32.4	31.5	30.6	29.7	28.9	27.3	25.9	24.6	23.4
15	7	217	98		52.4	48.6	45.4	42.4	39.7	38.4	37.2	36.1	35.0	34.0	33.0	32.0	31.1	30.3	29.4	27.9	26.4	25.1	23.8
15	10	220	100		53.2	49.3	46.0	43.0	40.2	39.0	37.8	36.6	35.5	34.5	33.5	32.5	31.6	30.7	29.8	28.2	26.8	25.4	24.2
16	0	224	102		54.1	50.2	46.8	43.7	41.0	39.7	38.4	37.3	36.2	35.1	34.1	33.1	32.1	31.2	30.4	28.8	27.3	25.9	24.6
16	3	227	103		54.9	50.9	47.4	44.3	41.5	40.2	39.0	37.8	36.6	35.6	34.5	33.5	32.6	31.7	30.8	29.1	27.6	26.2	24.9
16	7	231	105		55.8	51.8	48.3	45.1	42.2	40.9	39.7	38.4	37.3	36.2	35.1	34.1	33.1	32.2	31.3	29.7	28.1	26.7	25.4
16	10	234	106		56.6	52.5	48.9	45.7	42.8	41.5	40.2	38.9	37.8	36.6	35.6	34.6	33.6	32.6	31.7	30.0	28.5	27.0	25.7
17	0	238	108		57.5	53.4	49.7	46.5	43.5	42.2	40.9	39.6	38.4	37.3	36.2	35.1	34.1	33.2	32.3	30.6	29.0	27.5	26.1

growth chart for boys

How to use this chart

If you want to check your son is a healthy weight, first work out his BMI (see p25) and then plot it on the chart. Do not be tempted to interpret his weight from an adult BMI chart because children have different cut-off points and they vary between boys and girls – all of this is taken into account in this chart.

1. Find your son's age on the horizontal axis on the bottom or the top of the chart.
2. Work out his BMI (p25) and find the corresponding number on the left or right of the chart.
3. Trace a light vertical line from his age and a horizontal line from his BMI.
4. Find the point at which the two lines cross to discover whether he needs to gain weight, lose weight, or maintain his healthy weight. Check his BMI every 6 months to a year.

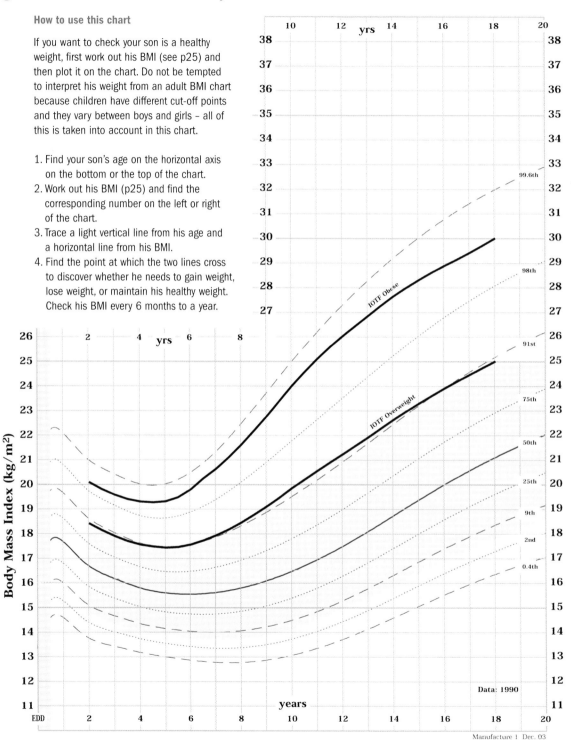

Data: 1990

Manufacture 1 Dec. 03

growth chart for girls

How to use this chart

If you want to check your daughter is a healthy weight, first work out her BMI (see p25) and then plot it on the chart. Do not be tempted to interpret her weight from an adult BMI chart because children have different cut-off points and they vary between boys and girls – all of this is taken into account in this chart.

1. Find your daughter's age on the horizontal axis on the bottom or the top of the chart.
2. Work out her BMI (p25) and find the corresponding number on the left or right of the chart.
3. Trace a light vertical line from her age and a horizontal line from her BMI.
4. Find the point at which the two lines cross to discover whether she needs to gain weight, lose weight, or maintain her healthy weight. Check her BMI every 6 months to a year.

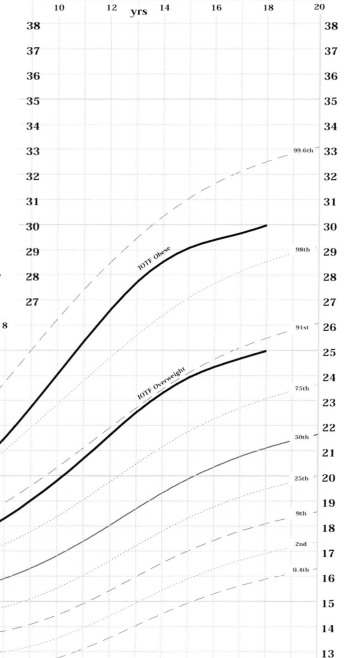

Data: 1990

Manufacture 1 Dec. 03

food and activity diary

The aim of the diary is to highlight eating patterns and to uncover triggers that lead you to overeat. You could also write down how much alcohol you are drinking so that you can keep tabs on it. Writing down your activities every day will give you a sense of achievement and encouragement to keep going! Tick off each glass of water you drink, too.

Monday

Time	Food/drink	Emotion	Hunger rating	Activity	Duration	Difficult/easy

Glasses of water drunk
eight 200ml glasses

calorie requirements

Here are the amounts of calories needed by an average person. Some people need more, such as sportsmen and women and very active individuals, and some people, such as those who are trying to lose weight, need less (see pp140–143).

Calories per day

Age	Males	Females
0–3 months	545	515
4–6 months	690	645
7–9 months	825	765
10–12 months	826	865
1–3 years	1,230	1,165
4–6 years	1,715	1,545
7–10 years	1,970	1,740
11–14 years	2220	1,845
15–18 years	2,755	2,110
19–50 years	2,550	1,940
51–59 years	2,550	1,900
60–64 years	2,380	1,900
65–74 years	2,330	1,900
75+ years	2,100	1,810

Calories per day

Pregnant women	
(final trimester)	+200
Breastfeeding women	
1 month	+450
2 months	+530
3 months	+570
4–6 months group 1	+480
4–6 months group 2	+570
6 months group 1	+240
6 months group 2	+550
group 1 = some breastfeeding	
group 2 = exclusively breastfeeding	

meal portion options

Use these portion guides, continued from pp34–35, to plan your eating and use portion control to monitor your food intake. You can keep your eating varied and balanced while you lose weight by choosing from this list to control your portions. See p156 for fruit and vegetable portions.

Bread, potatoes, pasta, and cereals

2 small oatcakes
3 small crackers or crispbreads
1 crumpet
½ English muffin
½ fruit or plain scone
1 Scotch pancake
1 small slice malt loaf
2 tbsp muesli
2 tbsp oats to make porridge
1 small chappatti
4 tbsp (teacup) plain popcorn

Milk, cheese, and yoghurt

1 small pot low-fat or diet yoghurt
1 glass low-fat milkshake or flavoured milk drink
80g (3oz) cottage cheese
60g (2oz) low-fat soft cheese
300ml (½ pint) skimmed milk

Meat, fish, and protein alternatives

2 boiled eggs (only 4–6 per week)
120g (4oz) soya, tofu, or vegetable-based meat alternative
4 tbsp cooked pulses such as beans, lentils, and dhal
60g (2oz) nuts

Fats and oils

1 tsp double cream
2 tsp single or soured or half-fat crème fraîche

Snacks

Snacking can be a valuable part of healthy eating and, surprisingly, eating for weight loss. If you do snack between meals when you are genuinely hungry, choose lower-fat foods when possible. When necessary, balance your total daily food intake by adjusting to smaller portions at meal times.

Approx. 50 calories

1 cup slimmers soup
1 cup low-calorie chocolate drink
1 biscotti
1 amaretto biscuit
Vegetables with 1 tbsp low-fat soft cheese or 2 tbsp salsa

Approx. 100 calories

1 fun-size chocolate bar
1 small pack low-fat crisps
1 slice toast with low-fat spread
1 crumpet with low-sugar jam
1 scoop sorbet

Approx. 150 calories

150g (6oz) low-fat yoghurt, custard, or rice pudding
1 smoothie
1 small packet crisps
1 chocolate biscuit
3 tbsp cereal with 200ml ($1/3$ pint) skimmed milk
1 plain or fruit scone with spread

Approx. 200 calories

2 fun-size chocolate bars
1 wholemeal rock bun
1 small slice fruit cake (no icing)
1 small bowl porridge
25g (1oz) peanut butter
1 large full-fat capuccino

daily fruit and vegetables

The UK Department of Health recommends eating five portions of fruit and vegetables a day – each portion is roughly equivalent to 80g (3oz). Choose from a wide range of possibilities – mix and match colour and texture for variety and optimum nutritional benefits.

Fruits

Apples, fresh	1 medium	Figs, fresh	2	Peach, dried	2 halves
Apples, puréed	2 heaped tbsp	Fruit juice	150ml (5fl oz)	Peach, fresh	1 medium
Apricots, dried	3 whole	Fruit salad, fresh	3 heaped tsp	Pears, fresh	1 medium
Apricots, fresh	3 apricots	Fruit salad, tinned	3 heaped tsp	Pears, tinned	2 halves
Apricots, tinned	6 halves	Fruit smoothie	150ml (5fl oz)	Pineapple, fresh	1 large slice
Avocado	½	Gooseberries	1 handful	Pineapple, tinned	2 rings
Bananas, fresh	1 medium	Grapefruit, fresh	½	Plums, fresh	2 medium
Blackberries	1 handful	Grapes	1 handful	Prunes, tinned	3
Blackcurrants	4 heaped tbsp	Kiwi fruit	2	Raisins	1 tbsp
Cherries, fresh	14	Lychees, fresh	6	Raspberries, fresh	2 handfuls
Cherries, tinned	1 heaped tbsp	Lychees, canned	6	Rhubarb, cooked	2 heaped tbsp
Clementines	2	Mango	2 medium slices	Rhubarb, tinned	5 chunks
Currants, dried	1 heaped tbsp	Melon	1 medium slice	Satsumas	2 small
Damsons	5–6	Mixed fruit, dried	1 heaped tbsp	Strawberries, fresh	7
Dates, fresh	3	Nectarine	1	Strawberries, tinned	9
Figs, dried	2	Orange	1	Sultanas	1 heaped tbsp
		Passion fruit	5–6	Tangerines	2 small

Vegetables

Ackee, tinned	3 heaped tbsp	Carrots, tinned	3 heaped tbsp	Parsnips	1 large
Artichoke	2 globe hearts	Cauliflower	8 florets	Peas, fresh	3 heaped tbsp
Asparagus, fresh	5 spears	Celery	3 sticks	Peas, frozen	3 heaped tbsp
Asparagus, tinned	7 spears	Chickpeas	3 heaped tbsp	Peas, sugarsnap	1 handful
Aubergine	⅓	Chinese leaves	⅕ head	Peas, tinned	3 heaped tbsp
Beans, broad, cooked	3 heaped tbsp	Courgettes	½ large	Pepper, fresh	½
Beans, butter, cooked	3 heaped tbsp	Cucumber	5cm (2in) piece	Pepper, tinned	½
Beans, French, cooked	4 heaped tbsp	Curly kale, cooked	4 heaped tbsp	Radishes	10
Beans, kidney, cooked	3 heaped tbsp	Karela	½	Spinach, cooked	2 heaped tbsp
Beans, runner, cooked	4 heaped tbsp	Leeks	1 (white parts only)	Spinach, fresh	1 cereal bowl
Beansprouts, fresh	2 handfuls			Spring greens, cooked	4 heaped tbsp
Beetroot, bottled	3 whole or 7 slices	Lentils	3 tbsp	Spring onions	8
		Lettuce (mixed leaves)	1 cereal bowl	Swede, cooked	3 heaped tbsp
Broccoli	2 spears	Mangetout	1 handful	Sweetcorn, baby	6
Brussels sprouts	8 heads	Mixed vegetables, frozen	3 tbsp	Sweetcorn, tinned	3 heaped tbsp
Cabbage, sliced	2 handfuls			Sweetcorn, on the cob	1 cob
Cabbage, shredded	3 heaped tbsp	Mushrooms, button	14	Tomato purée	1 heaped tbsp
Carrots, fresh, slices	3 heaped tbsp	Okra	16 medium	Tomatoes, fresh	1 medium
Carrots, shredded	⅓ cereal bowl	Onions, dried	1 heaped tbsp	Tomatoes, plum, tinned	2
		Onions, fresh	1 medium	Tomatoes, sundried	4 pieces

glycaemic index table

Food has a GI ranking from 0 to 100. Here are some examples of some common foods and their GI ratings. You can eat more low GI foods to control your blood glucose level, helping you to lose weight and stay healthy in many other ways (see pp122–123).

Low GI foods (55 or below)

Barley	25
Pulses, beans, and lentils	30–40
Apple and pear	38
Dried apricot	38
Low-fat yoghurt	15–30
Pasta, white and brown	32–50
Porridge	42
Fruit loaf	47
Pumpernickel bread	41
Grapefruit juice	48
Chocolate	49
White basmati rice	58
Bulghur wheat	48
Buckwheat	54
Porridge	42
Most vegetables	50
Oatmeal biscuit	54
Banana	55
Multi-grain bread	55

Medium GI foods (56–70)

Cakes	50–70
Muesli	56
Dried fruit	56–64
Honey	58
Plain biscuit	59
Pizza margharita	60
Muffin	60
Macaroni cheese	64
Couscous	65
Croissant	67
Taco shell	68
Chocolate and caramel bar	68
Wholemeal bread	69
Crispbread	69

High GI foods (70 and above)

White bread	70
Chips	75
Chocolate breakfast cereal	77
Jelly beans	80
Rice cake	82
Short-grain rice	85
Sticky rice	87
Iced biscuit	80
Rice pasta	90
French baguette	95
Sports energy drink	95

Lower GI meals and snacks

If you combine low GI foods with any high GI foods that you eat, you can reduce the overall effect on your blood glucose. Here are some examples of how to combine foods to keep your meals GI balanced.

Breakfast

Unsweetened fruit juice; porridge, muesli, or high-fibre cereal; wholegrain bread; low-fat milk or low-fat yoghurt

Lunch

Pasta with lots of vegetables; noodles or pitta bread filled with pulses; salad; wholegrain bread; baked beans, bean salad, or lentil soup

Evening meal

Fish or lean meat; vegetables; pasta, rice, noodles, cracked wheat, or sweet potato; peas, beans, lentils, or sweetcorn

Dessert

Apple, orange, cherries, pear, peach, grapes, or kiwi fruit with fruit yoghurt, low-fat custard, or fromage frais

Snacks

Apple, orange, cherries, pear, peach, grapes, or kiwi fruit with oatcakes, fruit loaf, or flapjacks

Index

Acknowledgments

About the author

Janette Marshall is the former Editor of *BBC Good Health* and *Tesco Healthy Living*. She was also Health Editor of eve magazine and a contributor to many national magazines and newspapers. Janette wrote *Fighting Fat, Fighting Fit* in association with the BBC health campaign. Her other titles include *The New Eat for Life* and other books that have won awards and commendations. Janette is a member of The Guild of Health Writers. She enjoys fitness, cooking, and sailing. **www.janettemarshall.co.uk**

The author would like to thank Bandolier for the BMI Chart; Tam Fry at The Child Growth Foundation for the Children's Growth Charts; Amanda Wynne and Lyndel Costain for their advice on the Personal Eating Plan; Alison Jeffery at the Early Bird study on diabetes in children; the press office at Sport England; and a special thanks to our consultant Dr Susan Jebb at MRC Human Nutrition Research.

Useful addresses

For more on how to take part in the **BBC's Big Challenge**, and to track your progress, find expert advice and inspirational ideas at **bbc.co.uk/bigchallenge**
Arthritis Research Campaign **www.arc.org.uk**
British Heart Foundation **www.bhf.org.uk**
British Nutrition Foundation **www.nutrition.org.uk**
British Dietetic Assoc. **www.bdaweightwise.com**
Cancer Research UK **www.cancerresearchuk.org**
Diabetes UK **www.diabetes.org**

Food Standards Agency **www.food.gov.uk**
National Healthy School Standard **www.wiredforhealth.gov.uk**
NHS smoking helpline **0800 169 0 169**
The Obesity Awareness and Solutions Trust **www.toast-uk.org.uk**
Obesity **www.nationalobesityforum.org.uk**
Quitline (smoking) **0800 00 22 00**
Weight Concern **www.shape-up.org**

Picture credits

p2 **Heike Löwenstein**; p8/9 **Heike Löwenstein**; p14 **DK Images**: Reuben Paris; p16 **Alamy**: BananaStock; p21 **Alamy**: BananaStock; p22 **DK Images**: Reuben Paris; p23 **DK Images**: Simon Brown; p24 **James Bell**; p26 **DK Images**; p31 **Alamy**: BananaStock; p32 **DK Images**: Anthony Johnson; p34/35 **DK Images**; p36 **Alamy**: Solstice Photography / Brand X Pictures; p37 **James Bell**; p38 **Alamy**: Jim Boorman / Pixland; p42 **DK Images**; p44 **Alamy**: ImageState Royalty Free; p46/47 **James Bell**; p50 **DK Images**: John Davis; p52 **DK Images**: Trish Gant; p54 **Alamy**: Ron Chapple / Thinkstock; p55 **James Bell**; p56/57 **James Bell**; p58 **Alamy**: Image100; p60/61 **DK Images**: Ian O'Leary; p64 **Alamy**: BananaStock; p66 **Alamy**: BananaStock; p68 **DK Images**: Simon Brown; p72 **DK Images**: John Davis; p73 **DK Images**: David Murray & Jules Selmes c; Clive Streeter cb, bc; p76 **DK Images**: Vanessa Davies;

p77 **Alamy**: Goodshoot; p81 **DK Images**: Simon Brown l; James Stevenson cr; p84 **DK Images**: Simon Brown; p86 **Alamy**: Tanya Constantine / Brand X Pictures; p88 **Alamy**: BananaStock; p90 **Alamy**: Big Cheese Photo; p94 **DK Images**: Vanessa Davies; p96 **DK Images**: Tim Ridley; p97 **DK Images**: Eddie Lawrence; p100 **Alamy**: BananaStock; p102 **Alamy**: BananaStock; p104 **Alamy**: Keith Brofsky / Brand X Pictures; p105 **James Bell**; p106 **Alamy**: Janine Wiedel Photolibrary; p108 **DK Images**; p110 **DK Images**: Reuben Paris; p112 **Alamy**: Xela; p114 **DK Images**: Trish Gant; p116 **Alamy**: BananaStock; p117 **James Bell**; p118 **DK Images**: Reuben Paris; p124 **DK Images**: Reuben Paris; p138 **DK Images**: Trish Gant; p139 **James Bell**; p140 **DK Images**: Ian O'Leary; p144 **Alamy**: Image Source; p150 **Alamy**: Paul Buckler / Pixland.
Jacket: **Heike Löwenstein**.